LESSONS
IN THE SCHOOL OF
PRAYER

AS TAUGHT BY

The Lord Jesus Christ Himself

Arranged and classified

with reference to their

original order

BY

ARTHUR T. PIERSON

www.solidchristianbooks.com

2015

Contents

Prefatory

The genesis of this book is very simple. Having occasion to prepare a special address on "Prayer," it occurred to me to collate and compare all the words spoken by our Lord himself upon the great theme, as it had often been found that His teachings upon any given subject, when so combined, constitute a consistent and harmonious whole— a body of doctrine, singularly comprehensive, and symmetrically complete.

In order to present His teachings, as to Prayer, most fully and satisfactorily, three things seemed essential: First, to gather them all together, for the sake of completeness; secondly, to classify them under appropriate divisions, for the sake of analysis and synthesis; and, thirdly, to arrange them as far as possible in chronological order, for the sake of discovering and disclosing any progress of doctrine which they might exhibit.

The result of these studies has proved so surprising and so satisfactory, that it is given to all devout students of the Scriptures, in the confidence that others will find here some such help, instruction, and comfort, as the writer has found. Perhaps even the imperfection of the work, here embodied, may incite other pupils of the Great Master to a more successful search into the wonderful words of Him who spake as never man spake.

ARTHUR T. PIERSON.

1127 Dean St., Brooklyn, New York.

OCTOBER, 1895.

I. OUR LORD'S OWN WORDS ON PRAYER.

I.

WHEN THOU PRAYEST,

Thou shalt not be As the hypocrites are;

For they love to pray, Standing in the synagogues,

And in the corners of the streets;

That they may be seen of men: Verily I say unto you,

They have their reward.

But thou,

When thou prayest,

ENTER INTO THY CLOSET;

And, when thou hast shut thy door,

Pray to thy Father,

Who is in Secret And thy Father,

Who seeth in secret,

Shall reward thee openly

II.

But, when ye pray,

USE NOT VAIN REPETITIONS,

As the heathen do;

For they think That they shall be heard,

For their much speaking-:

Be not ye, therefore, like unto them;

For your Father knoweth What things ye have need of,

Before ye ask Him.

III.

After this manner, Therefore, Pray Ye:

Our Father,

Who art in Heaven, Hallowed be Thy name,

Thy Kingdom come

Thy Will be done,

(On Earth, As it is in Heaven).

Give us, this day,

Our daily bread;

And forgive us our debts,

As we forgive our debtors; And lead us,

Not into Temptation;

But deliver us From evil;

For Thine is

(The Kingdom,

And the Power,

And the Glory,)

Forever.

Amen.

IV.

And, when ye stand praying,

Forgive,

If ye have aught against any;

That your Father also,

Which is in Heaven,

May forgive you your trespasses.

Love your enemies;

Bless them That curse you;

Do good to them

That hate you;

And pray for them

That despitefully use you,

And persecute you.

V.

HAVE FAITH IN GOD.

Verily I say unto you:

If ye have faith,

As a grain of mustard-seed,

Ye might say unto this sycamine-tree.

Be thou plucked up by the roots,

And be thou planted in the sea,

And it should obey you.

If ye have faith,

And doubt not,

Ye shall not only do this,

Which is done to the fig-tree,

But, also,

Whosoever shall say to this mountain,

Be thou removed,

And be thou cast into the sea;

And shall not doubt in his heart,

But shall believe

That those things which he saith

Shall come to pass,

He shall have whatsoever he saith.

And nothing shall be impossible unto you.

Therefore, I say unto you,

Whatsoever things ye desire,

When ye pray,

Believe that ye receive them,

And ye shall have them.

And all things,

Whatsoever ye shall ask in prayer,

Believing,

Ye shall receive.

VI.

And He spake a parable unto them,

To this end,

THAT MEN OUGHT ALWAYS TO PRAY

AND NOT TO FAINT,

Saying:

There was, in a city, a Judge,

Which feared not God,

Neither regarded man;

And there was a widow in that city,

And she came unto him, saying,

Avenge me of mine adversary!

And he would not, for a while;

But, afterward, he said, within himself,

Though I fear not God,

Nor regard man;

Yet, because this widow troubleth me,

I will avenge her;

Lest, by her continual coming,

She weary me.

And the Lord said:

Hear what the unjust Judge saith:

And shall not God avenge His own elect,

Which cry day and night unto Him;

Though He bear long with them?

I tell you, that He will avenge them speedily.

Nevertheless,

When the Son of man cometh,

Shall He find faith on the earth?

And He said unto them:

Which of you shall have a friend,

And shall go unto him, at midnight,

And say unto him,

Friend, lend me three loaves,

For a friend of mine, in his journey,

Is come to me,

And I have nothing to set before him;

And he, from within shall answer and say,

Trouble me not;

The door is now shut,

And my children are with me in bed;

I cannot rise and give thee:

I say unto you,

Though he will not rise and give him,

Because he is his friend;

Yet, because of his importunity,

He will rise, and give him

As many as he needeth.

And I say unto you:

Ask,

And it shall be given you;

Seek,

And ye shall find;

Knock,

And it shall be opened unto you.

VII.

If A SON shall ask bread

Of any of you that is A FATHER,

Will he give him a stone;

Or, if he ask a fish,

Will he, for a fish, give him a serpent;

Or, if he shall ask an egg,

Will he offer him a scorpion?

If ye then, being evil,

Know how to give good gifts

Unto your children,

How much more

Shall your heavenly father

Give the Holy Spirit

To them that ask Him!

VIII.

And He spake this parable,

Unto certain which trusted in themselves

That they were righteous,

And despised others.

Two men went up into the

Temple, To pray:

The one, a Pharisee,

And the other, a Publican.

The Pharisee stood,

And prayed thus with himself:

God, I thank Thee

That I am not

As other men are:

Extortioners, unjust, adulterers,

Or even as this Publican:

I fast twice in the week;

I give tithes of all that I possess.

And the publican, standing afar off,

Would not lift so much as his eyes unto heaven,

But smote upon his breast, saying:

God, be merciful unto me,

A sinner.

I tell you, this man went down to his house justified,

Rather than the other;

For every one that exalteth himself

Shall be abased;

But HE THAT HUMBLETH HIMSELF

SHALL BE EXALTED.

IX.

Again, I say unto you,

IF two of you shall agree, on earth,

As touching anything that they shall ask,

It shall be done for them,

Of my Father which is in Heaven;

For where two or three are gathered together,

IN my name,

There am I,

In the midst of them.

The Harvest is great,

And the laborers are few;

Pray ye therefore

The Lord of the Harvest,

That He would send forth laborers,

Into His Harvest.

X.

Whatsoever ye shall ask

IN my name

That will I do,

That the Father may be glorified

In the Son.

If ye shall ask anything,

IN MY NAME,

I will do it.

If ye abide in Me,

And my words abide in you,

Ye shall ask what ye will,

And it shall be done unto you.

Ye have not chosen me,

But I have chosen you;

And ordained you;

That ye should go and bring forth fruit,

And that your fruit should remain:

That whatsoever ye shall ask the Father,

IN MY NAME,

He may give it you.

Verily, verily, I say unto you,

Whatsoever ye shall ask the Father,

IN my name,

He will give it you.

HITHERTO have ye asked nothing,

IN my name,

Ask,

And ye shall receive;

That your joy may be full.

At that day ye shall ask IN my name;

And I say not unto you

That I will pray the Father for you;

For the Father Himself loveth you,

Because ye have loved Me,

And have believed

That I came out from God.

II. THE PROGRESS OF DOCTRINE.

The combined Testimony of the Four Gospel narratives is thus first presented, arranged as nearly as may be ascertained, in the order of utterance.

For the sake of exhibiting the mutual relations of all the members in this body of doctrine, regard is had to an obvious law of parallelism, which pervades it, and which helps to the apprehension of the minute beauty and symmetry of Christ's words; and hence the arrangement of parallel clauses as into the lines and stanzas of a poem, for there is a rhyme and rhythm of thought, as well as of words. That which appears to be the central lesson of each group is put in small capitals, to aid in fixing it in the mind; while words or phrases plainly intended to be in juxtaposition, as apposite or opposite to each other, are indicated by italics.

Thus, combining and arranging our Lord's own utterances and teachings on the subject of prayer, and, for the most part, in the actual order of their utterance so far as we can approximate to that order, we find that there is here a system of teaching: these scattered fragments, put together as they belong, form a mosaic. Moreover, they fall easily and naturally into ten groups, and a distinct process and progress of doctrine is perceptible, which will be the more apparent as these utterances are studied more closely.

We have sought to ascertain and exhibit their chronological order, because, so arranged, they reveal also a logical order, representing regular stages of advance, each lesson preparing the way for those which follow.

The central and controlling thought or theme in each of these ten groups, about which all the rest in that group crystallizes, may be expressed somewhat as follows:

16

Group I.—SECRECY WITH GOD, versus DISPLAY BEFORE MEN.

II.—QUALITY versus QUANTITY, as a standard of value.

III. —MATTER AND MANNER IN PRAYER.

IV. — FORGIVENESS VINDICTIVENESS TOWARD MAN.

V.—FAITH versus UNBELIEF TOWARD GOD.

VI.—IMPORTUNITY versus FAINTING, as to object sought.

VII.—FILIAL SPIRIT AND DIVINE FATHERHOOD.

VIII.—HUMILITY: SELF-ABASEMENT   versus   SELF-RIGHTEOUSNESS.

IX.—UNITY IN THE SPIRIT: AGREEMENT IN PRAYER.

X.—IN THE NAME OF CHRIST: IDENTITY WITH HIM.

There is thus one initial fundamental lesson on Secret Communion with God; then, two lessons on language, one cautioning against vain words, and the other, enjoining well-ordered words; then, three lessons on conditions of acceptable approach, such as a forgiving temper, faith in God's promise, and persistence in pleading; and, then, follow four lessons, on the higher secrets of prevailing power, such as a filial spirit toward the Father in Heaven, a self-abasing sense of sin, and dependence on grace, and identity with the Son of God, such as makes possible both individual and united prayer in His name.

In what follows,—remembering the importance of studying each group in its relations to what is manifestly its center of unity, namely, the thought which is meant to be controlling,—we shall seek simply to examine each word of our Lord, and discover its exact purport and purpose, as bearing upon the highest of all the arts of holy living, power to prevail in prayer. And, at the outset, let the reader join the writer, in supplicating the God of Prayer to illumine the mind for such devout and reverent study as shall disclose the hidden things of the Inspired Word:

"Unveil Thou mine eyes,

That I may behold wondrous things,

Out of Thy Law."—PSALM 119. 18.

CHAPTER I. CLOSET COMMUNION WITH GOD.

We are now prepared to study these lessons on prayer, in their order, and we must begin at the beginning; for in the school of Christ no second lesson is ever learned until the first has been. We ascend, as on the rungs of a ladder, one by one: to neglect or pass over one step forfeits progress.

"But thou,

When thou prayest,

ENTER INTO THY CLOSET."

This lesson of closet communion is the first taught, because in the order of time, of experience, of importance, it belongs first. Until this is thoroughly learned no other can be; and, in proportion as this is mastered, every subsequent teaching can and will be apprehended and appreciated. If therefore a disproportionate space seems to be assigned to this primary lesson, in our studies, it is because we find here the very foundation for all that follows.

Three things stand out prominently in this brief injunction, Enter into thy closet: first, the individual approach to God; second, the secret place of communion; third, the specific object, prayer.

The word, 'closet,' is unusual. The original Greek word, *tamelon*, is found but four times in the New Testament, in one place being rendered, 'secret chambers,' (Matt. 24.26) and in another, 'storehouse.' (Luke 12. 24) The words here used seem undoubtedly adapted from the Septuagint version of Isaiah 26. 20: "Come, my people, enter thou into thy chambers, and shut thy doors about thee."

There is also a marked emphasis on the singular number of the second personal pronoun. In the quotation from Isaiah, the opening call is plural, or collective, "Come, my people," but it immediately changes to the singular, "Enter thou into thy chambers"; and so, in our Lord's adaptation of these words, conspicuous stress is laid on the singular, "thou." Presently he adds a caution, perhaps as to prayers in which others publicly join, and says, "When pray"; but here how intensely individual: "But thou, when thou prayest, enter into thy closet; and when thou hast shut thy door pray to thy Father, who is in secret, and thy Father shall reward thee openly." Eight times, in these few words, is the singular pronoun used, and surely for some purpose.

How important, first of all, that we enter into the secret chambers of the divine meaning. What do these four words suggest: "Enter into thy closet"? The closet is simply a close, a closed place, shut in for privacy, shut out from intrusion and interruption. Christ was speaking to a Jewish audience and what would such language naturally suggest to such hearers? To the Hebrew mind there was one place that was preeminently a secret chamber: it was that in-most court of the Tabernacle and Temple, where God specially dwelt, and which was known as the Holy of Holies.

That was pre-eminently a secret chamber, a closed place. It had neither door nor window; unlike many an Oriental court which is open to the sky, it was roofed in and without skylight. It was never open: a door which we open, as we enter a room, we must close behind us; but, when the holiest of all was entered, the veil, raised as the High Priest went in, automatically fell back to its place as soon as it was released, and so kept the secrecies of God's chamber from mortal eyes.

Here then was one place, peculiarly marked by silence, secrecy, solitude and separation. Only one person ever entered here, at a time: "the High Priest, once every year, alone." Two persons were never known to meet there save himself and God. It was, in a unique sense, the place of which God could say, "Thou and I." It was the one great closet, shut-in place, secret chamber— the meeting place of one man and his Maker.

And, moreover, the one conspicuous, solitary article of furniture, there found, was the Mercy-Seat, the appointed meeting place, the basis of communion between the suppliant sinner and the merciful Hearer of Prayer. And thus the three conditions, suggested by the in-junction, 'Enter in thy closet,' met here as nowhere else: there was the secret chamber, the individual approach, and the mercy-seat for prayerful communion.

If we mistake not, we have now the key to this first lesson of our Lord on Prayer. The closet is the Holy of Holies where the suppliant soul meets God alone and communes with Him at the blood-sprinkled mercy-seat.

The highest act of prayer is impossible, unless and until the human suppliant deliberately seeks to meet God absolutely alone. To secure such aloneness with God we are bidden to 'enter into the closet,' to find some place and time where we may shut ourselves in with Him. This is so important that it is made emphatic by repeating the thought in another form: as though the word, closet, were not enough, Christ adds, "And when thou hast shut thy door, pray to thy Father, who is in secret" — a second word, meaning essentially the same as closet—a secret place.

Every praying soul needs some place and time for prayer, free from needless interruption and intrusion. The eye is mercifully furnished with an eyelid which instantly drops over the organ of vision, shutting out all external objects;

and, if the ear were similarly supplied with an eyelid, which could be used to shut out all sounds, as the eyelid does all sights, a closet could be instantly found and entered even in the midst of a throng, and the spirit might secretly commune with God, in the crowded streets or assemblies.

But, in the absence of any such natural provision for such complete seclusion and exclusion, our Lord counsels us, when we pray, to get somehow, somewhere, a silent, secret communing place with God, as the very basis of prayer, not only, but of all the holy living which is built upon prayer. The more completely we can separate ourselves from all other persons, all worldly pursuits and pleasures, all distracting cares or diverting thoughts, shutting out all else but God, the more perfect is the fitness of the hour and place to their purpose. And those who know how needful and helpful such secret times and places for prayer are, will secure, at any cost, the silent season even though, like the psalmist, it be found necessary to rise before others wake, and "prevent the dawning of the morning."

Yes, every praying soul needs to meet God absolutely alone. There are secrets of soul and spirit which no other human being however intimate ought to know, or indeed can know. (Psalm 119. 147).

"The heart knoweth his own bitterness;

And a stranger doth not intermeddle with his joy."
(Proverbs 14. 10)

We turn ourselves inside out to no other person, though it be a bosom friend: we would not if we could, we could not if we would. To the inmost secret chambers there is no open door; they are locked and sealed; words supply no key to them, and the seal of silence and secrecy is inviolable. But

22

"all things are naked and opened unto the eyes of Him with whom we have to do"; and therefore the closet, where we meet God alone and God only, is the one place for all such secrets. Nothing else will supply its place. The public service of worship, the more secluded 'family altar,' or the yet more private prayer in which only the husband and wife bow before God,—none of these can take the place of the solitary closet. There is at least one respect in which they, who are as 'one flesh,' are still 'twain'; for neither can ever fully know the other. But while, to our dearest and most intimate friend, we cannot reveal everything, from God, we can conceal nothing. His omniscient eye pierces to the secret chambers, despite the lock which no man can pick, the seal which no man dares break. God reads the thoughts which are yet "afar off," like forms faintly seen in the dim distance, and hears the word yet unspoken " in the tongue." And it is about these secret things which must be brought to the light in His presence, exposed, confessed, renounced, corrected before Him, that the closet is meant to give facility and freedom for converse with God. Hence this initial command to cultivate habitual aloneness with God. Like Jacob at Peniel, each suppliant must be "left alone" at times: the "thou" must be absolute and not the "ye," when the closet is entered.

Why now is such heavy stress laid, in our Lord's primary lesson on prayer, upon this shutting out of all else, and closing in of the suppliant with God?

Is it not, first of all, in order to what, as his "third instrument of Holy Living" Jeremy Taylor calls, The Practice of the Presence of God?

Nothing else has so marvelous an effect upon character and conduct, as this sense of God's Presence; and nothing is so difficult, nay impossible of attainment, so long as we neglect God's appointed means.

God is a Spirit, and must be worshipped in the spirit. Invisible to the eye, inaudible to the ear, intangible to the touch, He cannot be tested by the senses. They utterly fail us as channels of impression or communication. His subtle essence evades all carnal approach or analysis. He must be otherwise known, if at all: the spirit alone has the higher senses which, being exercised to discern good and evil, can enable us to perceive God and hold communication with Him. Hence, to those who live a sinful or even a worldly life, and are carnally minded, even the reality and verity of His existence become matters of practical, if not theoretical, doubt. There is a great deal of virtual atheism in mere unbelief. It is possible to recite the creed, "I believe in God, the Father Almighty," and yet never have had for one moment a real, true sense of the presence of God. Many may not deny that God is, but do they know that He is?

Such sense of the Divine Existence, such realization of the Divine Presence may be cultivated. God has appointed two means, and when used jointly they never fail: first a meditative reading of Holy Scripture, and secondly a habitual communion with Him in the closet. These two are in fact so closely related, that they are not only mutually helpful, but they operate upon us in ways almost precisely alike. Both introduce us into God's secret chambers.

When a devout disciple takes God's Word in his hands, for studious and thoughtful meditation, he naturally lifts his heart to Him who alone can unveil the eyes of his understanding to behold wondrous things out of His law. (Psalm 119. 18). As he reads and searches, meditating therein, the same Spirit who first inspired the Word, illumines his mind. New light is thrown upon the sacred page, so that what was obscure or hidden, becomes visible and legible; and new clearness of sight and insight is given to the spiritual organ of vision, so that it becomes more capable of seeing, more keen sighted and far-sighted.

Let those who have felt this double effect of the Spirit's teaching bear witness to the marvelous result. The Bible becomes a transformed book. It was before the best of all books, but it is now the Book of God—a chamber of disclosed mysteries—a house of many mansions, in which new doors constantly open into new apartments, massive and magnificent, God's art galleries, museums of curious things, treasuries of celestial gems. The devout student is filled with wonder, transported with delight. Words open with new meanings until we look through them into depths and heights, breadths and lengths, that are infinite. We are looking at a firmament which was before clouded—but the clouds are parting and heavenly constellations are visible. Meanwhile the eye has become telescopic, and where before we saw a few scattered stars, and an indistinct nebulous cloud, everything is ablaze with the glories of countless and many colored lights. When the Author of the Word becomes Instructor? And Interpreter of His own text-book, we read Heaven's great Classic with the notes and comments of the divine Author himself. And so he who devoutly searches the Scriptures, finds in them both eternal life and the testimony of Jesus; the reverent, searching, prayerful study of the Word of God is the cure of all honest doubt as to its divine origin, and the all-convincing proof of its plenary inspiration.

But, as the first Psalm teaches, he who would find such delight in the Law of the Lord, must meditate therein day and night. He must be a sort of sacramental tree of life, planted by the rivers of water. Mark the instructive, emphatic metaphor. The tree is permanently planted in the soil. Its roots are fixed organs of nutrition, constantly subordinate to the double purpose of growth and fruitfulness. Through the sponge lets at their extremities, the tree takes up the moisture of the river into itself, transmuting the water into sap, which deposits woody fiber in the branches and becomes juice in the fruit. The disciple is planted by the River of God,—the Word which goeth forth out of His mouth; he takes up into himself the very water of life, transmuting truth into character, and precepts and promises into practice. And so he who reads God's Word and, like the cattle that chew the cud, ruminates upon it, comes to know God through His Word, as we come to know men through their candid and self-revealing utterances. To meditate on God's words introduces us to the secret chambers of God's thoughts, and imparts insight into God's character. He becomes sure there is a God, who sees Him unveiled in the Scriptures, hears His still small voice in their audience chambers, traces His glorious footprints on their golden pavements; and, in times of temptation, trial, sorrow, doubt or any other need, God's words are so brought to his remembrance, and applied by the Spirit to his needs, that they become to such a reader, individually, God's words to him. He consults Holy Scripture as the oracles of God, and the oracles give answer. This is one of the closed mysteries, a stumbling-block of mysticism, or the foolishness of fanaticism, to the unbelieving; but, to him whose experience has been enriched by it, an open mystery, a fact as indisputable as anything in the realm of matter.

The other method of the practice of the Presence of God is communion with Him in the closet. And how like to the other is the process whereby prayer introduces us to His Fellowship! It implies meditation; it opens the secret chambers and reveals God; it discloses marvels and unlocks mysteries; it makes one sure that God "is and is a rewarded of them that diligently seek Him," (Hebrews 11. 6) which is the divinely declared condition of all acceptable, prevailing approach!

Upon this method of cultivating acquaintance with God, the great Teacher just now would fix our attention, as His primary lesson on Prayer. Let us seek to enter into the secret philosophy of this injunction: "Enter into thy closet; and when thou hast shut thy door, pray to thy Father who is in secret."

All other presence hinders the practice of the Presence of God. All thought of human auditors or observers is a hindrance to the closest approach and to the highest power in prayer. At the very moment when the supreme need is that all the faculties and activities of the being shall be gathered up, converged and concentrated, centralized and focalized as are scattered rays of light by a concave speculum or a convex lens, the mind is diverted and distracted, and the attention divided, by the thought that another human being hears or sees me. Any such divided attention must hinder the realization of the presence of the unseen God. Let us ask the reason why.

That profound lesson, taught to the Samaritan woman on the general subject of worship, includes prayer as one of the highest forms or acts of worship. God being a Spirit must be worshipped as such, and can be approached only by what is spiritual in man. There is such a thing among men as bodily contact and communion, as when hand joins hand, eye looks into eye, or words spoken by one's mouth reach another's ear. But, as God can neither be seen, heard nor touched, there can be no such contact between man and God. Being a Spirit, He can be approached only spiritually, that is by contact between our spirits and His.

In order to such contact, and in order that it may be real, recognized and conscious, all our spiritual faculties need to be active, on the alert; and all diversions or distractions of mind must be avoided which make impossible exclusive attention to the divine object of thought. But we are so constituted as to be unable to really fix attention on more than one thing at a time. Hence, in God's economy of Nature, many necessary acts are so provided for as to be half automatic, like the act of walking, and so only half conscious and semi-voluntary; for, were it necessary to concentrate all attention upon every step we take, we could, while walking, give heed to nothing else.

Moreover we find that we cannot fully exercise any one sense while the rest, or any one of them, is fully exercised and occupied: there is room for but one thorough sense-impression at a time. We cannot at the same moment fix our eyes upon a picture so as to study its effects in drawing and coloring, and yet give our ears to the hearing of a masterpiece of music, so as to observe critically its melody and harmony. Especially do we find that, to occupy the physical senses is so far to divert the mind from purely intellectual processes however simple.

For instance, in the late Harvard experiments in Psychology, where the test was made, how far an observer, watching rapid changes of color, could detect the delicate transitions from one shade to another, it was found that if, while so engaged, the simplest exercise in mental arithmetic were attempted, though it were only the addition or multiplication table, the power to discern these gradual changes of color was arrested. Man is so constituted that he can properly and thoroughly do but one thing at once.

Acquaintance with the unseen God is the first of all acquisitions. To attain the closest approach to Him, to get the most vivid sense of His presence, and so, the greatest power and blessing at the mercy-seat, all thought of men and of this world must be shut out, and all interruptions avoided that come through the senses or the imagination. So far only as we learn the art of thinking only of God, will this great lesson of closet prayer be learned, for, on the measure of our realization of the unseen Presence, all else must depend.

Our Lord's first lesson on prayer gives another hint of great value, though it is rather implied than openly expressed, for the more this injunction is studied the more it reveals of hidden meaning, itself a secret chamber whose mysteries are unveiled only to devout and persistent meditation.

He tells us that the Father who is in secret, or in the secret place, and who sees in the darkness of the soul's Holy of Holies, rewards the suppliant openly— 'in the open.' Here again we are reminded of the High Priest's approach to the mercy-seat. When he went into the holiest of all, with blood of atonement, it is neither recorded nor intimated that he was there wont to offer up supplication; certainly the element of petition is nowhere prominent. He seems to have gone in thither, rather to 'appear before God'—simply to present himself, with the blood, before the mercy-seat,—his presence constituting his plea; and the blood of atonement, both the sign of his obedience and the pledge of his acceptance. There he seems to have waited before God, not so much to offer up prayers and supplications, as to receive from God impressions and revelations.

The yet unexplained mystery of the Urim and Thummim may have some connection with this revealing of God's mind and will. The most plausible interpretation of this mystery is perhaps that which suggests that the Light of the Shekinah fire, shining on the breast-plate of the High Priest, made successive letters, of the names with which its stones were graven, to stand out conspicuous, so that he could in characters of light spell out the divine message. And it is a curious fact that the twelve names with which the sacred stones were marked, taken together, contain almost every letter of the Hebrew Alphabet!

However this be, the Mercy-Seat was to the High Priest mainly a place, not of petition but of communication, of impartation from God, of divine revelation. He waited there, for a message which he bore back to the people in benediction.

Certain it is that the closet is not an oratory—a place for prayer in the narrow sense of mere request—so much as an observatory, from which to get new views of God, and new revelations of Him. There is a quest higher than mere request—a search after knowledge of God and communication from Him. In this secret place, devout souls learn what is meant by communion—and communion is mutual. There is not only prayer offered, but blessing received. The praying soul speaks to God, and hears God speak. He who enters the closet gets as well as gives, and finds the most precious part of this communion, not in any requests imparted Godward, but in returns imparted manward, the reception from God of divine impressions and communications. The reward, promised, comes while yet he speaks and waits before the Lord: believing he receives, and receiving enjoys. Such reward cannot be kept secret. It makes the heart to overflow and even the face to shine.

True prayer, in its highest form and reach, is not only imperative but receptive: the whole nature going out to God in adoration, thanksgiving, confession, supplication, intercession; but also opening all its channels for the incoming of blessing. Communion becomes intercommunication—Jacob's Ladder rests in the closet and reaches to the Throne—and angels descend to bring blessing, as well as ascend to bear petition; or, as a simple Japanese convert put it, prayer is like the well where one bucket comes down while the other goes up, only that in this case it is always the empty bucket that goes up and the full one that comes back.

Of this aspect of prayer, as a revelation of God to the suppliant, the current definitions of prayer seem to take little if any notice. For example the Westminster standards define prayer as "the offering up of our desires unto God, in the name of Christ, by the help of His Spirit, with confession of our sins and thankful acknowledgment of His mercies." (Larger Catechism, Q. 178). Full as is this definition, it has no recognition of that element in prayer which involves meditative communion with the Divine Presence for the sake of a present communication from God to the soul.

With most praying people, the fundamental if not the exhaustive conception of prayer is asking somewhat of God. This is indeed a part, but surely it is not the whole, of prayer; and it may be doubtful whether more than a beginning is made unless and until there be a disclosure of God to the soul. We read of our blessed Lord himself that at times he withdrew from all human companionships, for the purpose of secret communion with the Father; as when he went out "into a mountain to pray and continued all night in prayer to God." These midnight, all-night interviews, mark the great crises of his life on earth; and it cannot be supposed that he spent all these hours in continuous supplication. Was it not rather like Gideon, on the plains of Jezreel, to spread out his whole being like fleece, to drink in the heavenly dew in the Father's Presence and in the strength of this celestial nectar confront new trials and temptations?

31

Thus meditative prayer, like reflective reading of the Word of God, becomes a perpetual means and medium of communion with God, and so, also, of Revelation of God, for communion not only leads to, but itself becomes and is, revelation. He who converses with a friend, habitually, has no room for doubt as to that friend's existence and presence; and God meant that this simple method of converse with Himself should be a demonstration that He is, and is a Rewarder of them that diligently seek Him—a demonstration so convincing as to dispel all doubts, being itself the sufficient proof of His reality and verity as the ever present, living, helping God.

The humblest believer, however unlettered or unlearned, may attain in this school of prayer to practical certainty in divine things; he needs not to read volumes of Apologetics, or Evidences of Christianity: let him but cultivate the sense of the Presence of God, and the proofs, though he cannot always formulate them for others, become convincing and overwhelming to himself. Indeed we oftenest find such assurance of faith in the humbler, simpler sort of disciples; and, because it is found in the ignorant and unlearned rather than the princes of this world, or the great scholars of the church, there is a proneness to associate such faith with credulity and even with superstition, as in that abominable lying maxim, "Ignorance is the mother of devotion." But wrongly; for while the more intelligent and intellectual too often lean to their own understanding, and turn to human logic and philosophy for confirmation of their faith, he who, being untaught of men and having little access to books, has no other means of strengthening his assurance save converse with God, is compelled to learn in God's school, where logic and philosophy are never perverted to the purposes of fallacy and sophistry. "He that dwelleth in the secret place of the Most High, abides under the shadow of the Almighty"; and the darts of satanic doubt can pierce him, only as they first pass through the divine "Wings" which are his covering and shelter.

Here, then, is the initial lesson of our Lord upon Prayer. And, as in any other first lesson, a master teacher naturally lays down fundamental laws or first principles, we find here laid the cornerstone of all true prayer. This primary lesson is so easy to see that it is hard to mistake, namely: Prayer is at bottom *the meeting of a human suppliant, alone with God for supplication and communion at the mercy-seat, and revelation of the Existence, Presence and character of God.*

It is plain why the preliminary caution of the Great Teacher is directed against hypocritical ostentation. "When thou prayest, thou shalt not be as the hypocrites are; for they love to pray, standing in the synagogues and in the corners of the streets that they may be seen of men. Verily I say unto you, they have their reward." In praying, as in almsgiving and fasting, hypocrisy courts publicity. Through all this warning about doing righteousness,' (See Matt. 6. 1, R. V). the one emphatic phrase is—"to be seen of men." The hypocrite's prayer is addressed to a human audience rather than offered to the divine ear. It has reference mainly to outward appearance and transient impression. Hence publicity is an object; and in the synagogues where the crowd's throng, at the street corners or crossways where all points of the compass are commanded at once, the hypocrites took their stand that they might be seen of men. The formalist may not be a hypocrite, but his mind is taken up with the externals, and here again "the letter killeth," and only "the spirit giveth life."

Christ would teach praying souls, and have them learn first of all, that this being seen of men is to be avoided rather than courted and sought. To concentrate all thought and desire upon God, to forget all else in order not to forget Him, and so to be lost in the absorbing sense of His presence — this is the first secret of power in prayer, and in fact the secret also of all power in holy living and serving.

This first lesson is also the last, for there is no higher, nobler fruit of habitual closet communion with God than this new sense of divine realities. Paul gently rebukes the Hebrew Christians because they have not, by reason of use, exercised their senses, trained them to keenness, to discern good and evil. (Hebrews 5. 12). Of course he does not refer to physical senses, whose office is not the discerning of moral qualities. The spirit has its senses, as well as the body, and they are trained to acuteness and exactness by holy exercise. Imagination is the sense of the unseen; Reason, the sense of truth and falsehood; Conscience, the sense of right and wrong; Sensibility, the sense of the attractive and repulsive; Memory, the sense of the past. The understanding and heart have eyes with which to see God's beck and glance, ears with which to hear His still small voice, organs of touch wherewith to "Handle" Him and see that is He Himself. The closet is the grand school for the education of these senses. There we go to get enrapturing visions, looking at things unseen, eternal; to listen intently and hear the divine whisper; to catch the scent of heavenly gardens; to taste and see that the Lord is good. And it is to reach such results, that we need aloneness with God, that He may hold our senses fixed upon Himself.

These words of our Lord, 'Enter into thy closet,' supply a key to many mysteries of Scripture biography. We unlock Jacob's experience at Bethel — "Surely God was in this place and I knew it not; this"—a desert place with a stone pillow —"is none other but the house of God, and this is the gate of Heaven": and particularly, at Peniel, later on, when he saw 'the face of God' and got a lifelong blessing, and the supplanter of men became the prince of God. Yes, it is when we are "left alone" that great revelations come. Elijah was bidden to 'Hide' himself, and then 'Shew' himself unto Ahab: it was the hiding that made the shewing such a power in Israel. When Elisha 'went in and shut the door upon them twain and prayed unto the Lord," (2 Kings 4. 33). there came out from that secret chamber the child of the Shunammite brought back to life. Nathanael under the fig-tree was without doubt holding secret converse with God; and, when Christ said to him, "Before that Philip called thee, when thou wast under the fig-tree I saw thee" the guileless Israelite of Cana recognized in the Christ before him one whom he had met in the secret place, and who now as then read his thoughts.

To get such exalted impressions of God, in closet communion, there is needful the Time-element. A rapid glance leaves a comparatively transient impression; but a gaze, which takes time to fix itself on an object, so takes in its whole impress as to leave its image permanently in the mind.

It is true, as our Lord warns us, that we are not heard for our much speaking: it is not many words or long prayers that prevail. But it is nevertheless also true that haste or hurry in prayer defeats the main end in view, preventing that calmness, concentration, peace and rest—that quiet of soul which helps to the divine revelation. There is an ethical suggestion in that word reflective, so often applied to a temperament or spiritual mood, and so inseparable from true devotion: it suggests a power to reflect as in a mirror, divine verities and realities. To all such reflection hurry and worry are fatal. He who rushes into the Presence of God, to hasten through a few formal petitions, and then hasten back to outside cares and pursuits, does not tarry long enough to lose the impression of what is without, and get the impress of what is within, the secret chamber. He does not take time to fix his mind's gaze on the unseen and eternal. Many a so-called 'praying man' has never once really met and seen God in the closet. The soul, disturbed and perturbed, tossed up and down and driven to and fro by worldly thoughts and cares, can no more become a mirror to reflect God, than a ruffled lake can become the mirror of the starry heights that arch above it. He who would look downward into his own heart-depths and see God reflected there, must stay long enough for the stormy soul to get becalmed. Only when He first gives peace is the nature placid enough to become the mirror of heavenly things.

But when such communion becomes real, prayer ceases to be mere duty and becomes delight. All sense of obligation is lost in privilege. Love seeks the company of its object, simply for the sake of being in the presence of the beloved one; as one little fellow explained his quietly coming into his father's study by the hunger for his presence—"just to be with you, papa." Have any of us not known what it is to cultivate companionship for its own sake, mutely sitting in the presence of another whom we devotedly love? And do we not love God enough to make it an object to shut ourselves in with Him at times just to enjoy Him? Is there no taint of selfishness in the prayer which knows no other, not to say higher, motive than to ask for some favor? Jude counsels us to 'pray in the Holy Ghost' as a means whereby we keep ourselves in the love of God, as Archbishop Usher, in his last days, when animal heat failed him, kept himself in the warm sunshine. He who knows the very ecstasies of the secret chamber, there learns to keep himself in the love of God, finding therein the Sunbeam whose light illumines, whose love warms, whose life quickens. God's Presence becomes the atmosphere he breathes and without which his spiritual life cannot survive. Such a habit of abiding in the Presence of God, and dwelling upon His glorious perfections develops a holy and enamoring love, which can only say with Zinzendorf and Tholuck, "I have but one passion: and it is He and He alone!"

It has been already hinted, in passing, that such God-revealing habits of prayer lay the very corner-stone of all holy living.

There is nothing vital to godliness that is not nourished on closet air. Prayer is spiritual respiration and the secret place furnishes its oxygen and ozone.

For example, what a power both to reveal and to prevent Sin is this Sense of the Presence of God which is trained in secret prayer.

We must not be surprised if the communion with God that reveals Him unveils ourselves. 'Whatsoever doth make manifest is light.' And if we linger long before that Shekinah fire, which makes the golden wings and faces of the cherubim's shine, it will pierce through every disguise and show us the very thoughts and intents of the heart. The sword of flame will pierce to the dividing asunder of soul and spirit. Secret prayer is always a revelation of self as well as of God. We must be content to endure its searching ray, and even to invoke it.

"Search me, O God, and know my heart;

Try me and know my thoughts;

And see if there be in me any wicked way,

And lead me in the everlasting way." (Psalm 139. 24)

Daniel was so faultless that even enemies could find nothing in him to accuse save his faith in God and his unceasing prayer; yet, in the presence of the searchlight of that Glory, he beheld even his "comeliness turned into corruption." Isaiah in that Presence, cried, "Woe is me; for I am a man of unclean lips and dwell in the midst of a people of unclean lips; for mine eyes have seen the King, the Lord of Hosts" (Isaiah 6. 5). Peter, under such self-exposure, fell down at Jesus' knees, saying, "Depart from me, for I am a sinful man, O Lord!" (Luke 5. 8). But all such self-revelation and self-condemnation only brings blessing, for it is the result of a divine vision! The divine answer to such human self-abasement is a new communication and exaltation. Daniel abhors himself, but hears a voice saying, "O Daniel, a man greatly beloved, fear not; for from the first day that thou didst set thine heart to understand and to chasten thyself before thy God, thy words were heard and I am come for thy words." (Daniel 10. 8-12). Isaiah bewailed his unclean lips, but the seraph touched those same lips with a live coal from off God's altar, and said, "Lo, this hath touched thy lips, and thine iniquity is taken away, and thy sin is purged." (Isaiah 6. 7). Even Peter, who felt so unfit for the companionship of the Lord that he involuntarily besought Christ to depart from him, heard only the assuring answer, "Fear not, from henceforth thou shalt capture men alive."! (Luke 5. 10).

The sense of the Divine Presence, which reveals sin, also prevents it. When Joseph was in the crisis of awful temptation his answer to the syren voice of the tempter was an obvious sign of his habit of thinking of God. He had evidently learned that great truth, "Thou, God, seest me!" He practiced the Presence of God, and it was natural to say with himself, "How can I do this great thing and sin against God?" And, when Paul rises to the height of his grand argument on personal holiness, he reminds Corinthian Christians that they are the very temple (vaos)—the Holy of Holies, of God; and that the Spirit of God dwelleth in them. And, on the basis of this awful fact, he builds that exhortation, "Having therefore these promises, let us cleanse ourselves from all filthiness of the flesh and spirit, perfecting holiness in the fear of God." (2 Cor. 6. 4-7. i.) What a security in the hour of temptation, however sudden, overwhelming, and otherwise irresistible, is the thought, the conviction, the consciousness, "Thou, God, seest me. I can go nowhere without Thy Presence. The wings of the morning are not swift enough, nor the uttermost parts of the earth far enough, to remove me from Thine Eye and Thine Hand." Such are the profound, devout meditations of that Psalm of the Presence of God (Psalm 139) which cannot be surpassed for poetry or piety. How natural and easy, when one feels God near, searching the inmost depths of being with omniscient glance; so near that He can never be afar off, but by omnipresent companionship is with us because in us, everywhere; and with omnipotent energy creating, upholding, strengthening—how easy and natural to do what pleases God, and say to seductive allurements of evil, "My heart is fixed." It is only when a saint loses the sense of God's Presence that voluntary sin can be possible.

Again, what intrepid courage in witnessing for God, and following the path of heroic duty, this sense of the Presence of God imparts.

Elijah, the stern reformer of abuses, the great rebuker of idolatry among the people and of iniquity in high places, cultivated this consciousness of God. His habitual and characteristic phrase was, "Jehovah, God of Israel, before whom I stand"—as though he felt himself to be constantly standing in the presence of his Divine Master—a servant whose eyes were to the eye and hand of that Master, watching and waiting to be guided by a beck or even a glance. It was because he stood before God, as one who awaits orders and receives from His very mouth his messages, that he could stand unabashed before Ahab and Jezebel.

In the old days of the Commonwealth it was customary to open the Connecticut Legislature with what was known as an 'election sermon.' On one occasion the chosen preacher was one of the famous brothers Strong, a man whose modesty was equal to his merit, and who shrank from the grave responsibility. On the way to the place of assembly, as he walked beside his brother, who was also a minister of the gospel, this retiring man disclosed his oppressive burden of reluctance to face such a body of distinguished men, among whom would be found lawyers and barristers and judges, generals and statesmen, doctors of divinity and doctors of law, governors and ex-governors, the very flower of the Commonwealth. "How can I venture before such an audience?" said he to his brother. "You have only to remember," answered he, "that in that hall of assembly is ANOTHER PRESENCE, SO supremely august, that in comparison all other presence becomes utterly insignificant and contemptible, and preach as in that Presence alone." Keeping before him this thought, he went fearlessly to the discharge of his solemn duty, and all un-wholesome restraint was gone. Rev. Dr. Samuel H. Cox recalled this incident when called to the momentous crisis of his life, addressing the Evangelical Alliance with its representatives of all nations, and the thought of that same Presence nerved his fainting spirit.

So went John Baptist before Herod, Paul before Agrippa, Felix, Nero; Luther before the Diet of Worms, Knox before Queen Mary. And was it not this same sense of the Father's

Presence, who never left him alone, which made Him whom the prophet called 'The Servant of Jehovah,' to go with such infinite calmness before Herod and Caiaphas and Pilate? Who was ever so utterly careless of human opinion, indifferent alike to censure or applause, because he could say, 'I do always those things which please Him!' When his disciples, after one of his severe rebukes of the Pharisees for making void the commandments of God through their tradition, said, "Knowest thou that the Pharisees were offended after they heard this saying," He calmly answered, "Every plant which my Heavenly Father hath not planted shall be rooted up." (Matt. 15. 12, 13). He could not accommodate his message to the hearer, but the hearer must accommodate himself to the message. And so will every true messenger of God answer human opposers, if he is wont to cultivate and cherish the sense of the Presence of God.

This practice of the Presence of God is the secret of both fidelity and cheerfulness in the discharge of common duty.

Whatever is a help to holy living must be found in those secret chambers to which devout study of the Word and habitual communion with a prayer-hearing God open the doors. Any burden can be borne, any trial endured, any responsibility assumed, when this sense of God is active and constant. To be about his "Father's business" was the secret of our Lord's untiring service and unalloyed satisfaction; and with what patient hope do we work out the mission of a complete life, while we feel that God works in, to will and to do!

That is a deep law of life which Paul puts in those few words in his first letter to Corinth: (I Cor. 7. 20-24) "Let every man, in that calling wherein he is found, therein ABIDE WITH GOD." When the renewing grace of God finds a man engaged in an honest calling however humble, he has no need to change his vocation, but only to take a new and divine Partner, and henceforth abide with God in his daily sphere of work. How simple, how sublime! Christ wrought at the bench of the carpenter of Nazareth until at thirty years of age he entered on his public ministry, as though to teach us that no workman need be ashamed of his craft when he follows it as God's servant; and that, whether it be the bench of the carpenter or the shoemaker, or the bench of the judge; the loom of the weaver, the wheel of the potter, or the desk of the author, the studio of the artist, the throne of the emperor—any place where service is rendered to God becomes a pulpit of witness, a shrine of God.

A humble monk known as Brother Lawrence has left behind a few simple letters that have awakened profound interest. ("The Practice of the Presence of God.")

From these letters it appears that, being called to the menial office of a cook in a convent, he was led, by this suggestion of Jeremy Taylor's, to cultivate the habit of thinking of God as ever with him, and as a partner in his lowly calling, until it became easier to think of Him as present than as absent; and until that convent kitchen became as another garden of Eden, and every day as one of the days of Heaven upon earth.

We are now prepared to understand why and how this sense of the Divine Presence is especially and in every way so helpful to prayer that in exact proportion to its vividness and constancy is prayer effective and powerful.

Every element and exercise of prayer is dependent upon it. It prompts the highest outburst of thanksgiving, for it reveals the fact that God is and reveals Him as He is: we get in the secret place glimpses of the character and glory of God which are the very inspiration of gratitude. To know what God is, is of far more consequence than to know what He does. God is Love, and therefore all His outgoings are lovely and loving: the stream is as the spring.

We have seen that to realize the Divine Presence leads to most heart-searching contrition and confession, because in the light of His purity and holiness sin's enormity and deformity are most clearly seen; and in the contrast of the glory of His goodness our unworthiness and un-gratefulness become awfully apparent. And, in like manner, when the mind is filled with new views of God, His truth and grace, the reality and verity of His promise, our supplications and intercessions become the confident appeals of suppliants who "have boldness and access with confidence by the faith of Him." (Eph. 3. 12; compare Hebrews 4. 16).

There is thus no side or aspect of true prayer which this vision of God in the closet does not touch. Contemplation of God compels contemplation of self; a new sense of destitution, degradation, depravity; a deeper contrition, a sincerer confession; a more importunate entreaty—a new repentance toward God, a new faith in God, a new separation unto God, a new power with God.

The loftiest conception of Prayer is that which finds expression in what is called worship—worth-ship—the ascribing of worth to God, describing His worth in the highest expressions of praise, inscribing His worth on the forefront of the mitre, the palms of the hands, the door-posts of the house, and the gates whereby we go out and in— keeping before us and others the infinite excellence of God. Worship is more than thanksgiving and praise, for it includes both; and it rises above both in adoration, the whole soul and spirit going out to Him in devout words, or more likely in groaning's and raptures which cannot be

43

uttered, the mute language of emotions and affections which have no adequate articulate, human dialect.

Worship is the form of Prayer which fills Heaven, and echoes in the Apocalypse when the door is opened into Heaven: "Thou art WORTHY, O Lord!" Redeemed throngs and even angelic hosts, lost in the vision of infinite excellence and worthiness, rest not day or night from such adoration. Surely to get a new apprehension and appreciation of these adorable perfections is the ideal of Prayerful Communion.

In the Psalm of Nature (Psalm 29.), all creation is seen to be God's Temple. Nature is the vast cathedral where He is throned, and all the forces of the material universe are vocal with His praise. The boom of the great waters sounds the deep diapason, the gentle breezes breathe melodies, and the peal of the thunders rolls its pedal bass, while cyclones and whirlwinds add majesty to the chorus. Lightnings flash like electric lamps, and giant oaks and immortal cedars bow like worshippers. In this Psalm of Nature it is declared that "In His Temple, everything doth shout GLORY!" (Verse 9 (Hebrew)).

To those devout souls that abide in the secret chambers with God, the closet it expands into a grand cathedral. Every power and faculty of body, mind, soul and spirit shout 'Glory!' Memory brings her grateful stores to lay them at God's feet; Imagination, the poet and painter, weaves choicest tributes and paints glorious pictures, as aids to Faith;

Reason, the logician, constructs its most eloquent arguments to set forth God's claim on universal homage and love; Understanding, overawed before the Infinite mind, can only mutely confess its own insignificance; Conscience, the Judge, pronounces Him perfect in all moral beauty; the Will, the Sovereign of man, lays down its imperial sceptre at His feet who is alone worthy to rule; and Affection, despairing of ever responding fully to such perfect love, breaks her alabaster flask and fills the whole house with the odor of her anointing. The soul that knows the closet's revealing can only say, "Who is like, O Lord, unto Thee!"

It is because our Lord would teach us how to reach these lofty heights of heavenly experience that he makes his first lesson on Prayer, Enter into thy closet. The first rung in the ladder of ascent is faith in the actuality, reality, verity of the divine existence. And hence, as the primary condition of prayer, we are told, "he that cometh to God must believe that He is (that He exists), and is a rewarder of them that diligently seek Him." Of what use indeed to pray— nay, what but an affront, rather than an approach, to God—if we do not believe that He exists; and what is the closet for, if not to cultivate those spiritual senses which alone can perceive Him and receive Him?

We dared not leave this first lesson until we had taken time thoroughly to master it, that we might so understand those which follow. These may therefore be treated more briefly, as the first throws light over all the remaining path to be trodden. But let us not dismiss this primary lesson without once more recalling and impressing its commanding truth, that communion with God is the essential secret of all holiness of character, conduct and service; and that meditation on the divine character and perfections prepares us not only for prevailing supplication but for reception of divine blessing. Let us think of the secret chamber as a place of vision—of contemplation of God, which makes possible new impressions, new discoveries into His nature, new revelations of His goodness, new impartations of His power. Thus it comes to pass that before we call He answers, and while we are yet speaking He hears. (Isaiah 65. 24). Communion proves mutual—an outgo, and an income, a Voice that answers as well as a voice that cries.

What a new factor in our spiritual life would such Prayer prove!

The most devout souls have found it not only profitable but natural to make the first exercise in closet devotion mute meditation. In the Prayer of Habakkuk we have a hint that this is becoming to all true worship:

"The Lord is in His Holy Temple!

Let all the earth keep silence before Him." (Habakkuk 2. 20).

And when, in the Apocalypse, that most wonderful vision of the prayers of saints is about to be disclosed—the mysterious announcement which precedes it is:

"There was SILENCE in Heaven about the space of half an hour," (Rev. 8. 1.)

as though such silence were the only fit prelude and preparation for a revelation of such magnificence and significance.

God is here; but what if I know it not? Let me tarry till I do know it. Then how much added power will come into my communing, and with what new anointing shall I go forth to life's work, and witness and warfare!

CHAPTER II. THE MATTER, MANNER AND SPIRIT OF PRAYER.

"WHEREWITH shall I come before the Lord?" is the natural question which the suppliant asks. How shall we render "the calves of our lips," so that they shall be unblemished and acceptable on the altar of prayer and praise?

The second and third lessons in this series have so close a relation, both logically and chronologically, that we hesitate to separate them. The former of them is negative: "Use not vain repetitions as the heathen do"; the latter is positive: "After this manner therefore pray ye." In one case there is a warning against many and vain words; in the other there is an example, model, or mould of prayer, couched in words so singularly few, elect, and select, that nothing could be omitted or added without marring the symmetry of the most perfect form of prayer ever devised; one in which the language used is so far from being either "vain" or repetitious that it is infinitely full of meaning, each word being pregnant with significance.

II. Unmistakably does our Lord teach that the power of prayer does not depend on a multitude of words. We are not heard for our "much-speaking." Nor are we under the necessity of endless explanation and expansion, as though we were dealing with one who is ignorant of our needs, or incapable of understanding our words. Our Heavenly Father knoweth, before we ask Him, what things we have need of; and reads our hearts' desire even through the most imperfect medium of utterance; nor does He need, like a city held in a state of siege, to be constrained or compelled to grant our requests, as though His unwillingness, indifference or aversion must be first overcome. Like as a father pitieth his children, does He pity us; and earthly parents do not yearn over their offspring as He does over His own.

Our Lord's caution seems mainly directed against all mere empty repetition —"vain repetitions," such as abound in heathen prayers, wherein much speaking is supposed to make up for the lack of acceptable asking—a practice which finds both example and illustration in the experience of Elijah with the priests of Baal on Mount Carmel. (I Kings 18. 26).

The warning against vain repetition has a wider application: it takes in all thoughtless words and careless forms in prayer. The moment any set form of words is adopted, and begins to be familiar, so that it can be repeated thoughtlessly like the alphabet or multiplication table, we run the risk of vain repetitions. The Thibetan is not the only worshipper who turns a prayer-wheel, or reels prayer off by the yard. It is possible to recite a prayer, no less sublime than the model which Christ gave his disciples, and yet with so little thought, understanding, appreciation or emotion, that it becomes automatic and mechanical. Was it not Luther who said that the Lord's Prayer is the principal martyr because it has suffered so much and so often from thoughtless repetition?

Those who use liturgical forms in worship have to be perpetually on their guard against the danger of losing out of the forms the spirit of true devotion, and of swinging an empty censer before the Lord. And it is itself a historic warning that, in proportion as spiritual life and power decline in the church, forms multiply and usurp the place of spontaneous and free worship. In the more spiritual periods of revival—of renaissance of holy living—devout disciples involuntarily burst these bonds, as a chrysalis does its shell when its wings are ready for a flight. While life is low, there is perhaps a contentment with inaction and restraint; but, when souls come forth into true freedom, like Lazarus from the grave, they must be loosed and let go. Inflexible forms are like swaddling-clothes or embalming-cloths; they will do for babes or for lifeless people, but, in proportion as regenerate disciples attain unto the liberty of the Spirit, they speak as He gives them utterance. To say no more, the most devout men and women have confessed that, in their highest experiences of drawing near to God, they are hampered and hindered by set forms of prayer; and that, in order to prevent even the best forms from becoming vain and empty, they must keep perpetually studying to enter more fully into their meaning and spirit, as, for example, in the use of the Lord's Prayer.

III. As to the manner of Prayer. While our Lord here presents a form or mould for supplication, there is no sign that He meant to prescribe it as a form, above all as a fixed form of words to be used on all occasions or within any exclusive limits. It would seem to have been suggested first by a request from His disciples: "Lord, teach us to pray as John also taught his disciples." But for this request, the "Lord's Prayer" might never have been. Certainly it cannot legitimately be pressed into the service of ritualism, or made a barrier to freedom of utterance in supplication.

It teaches this, and not of necessity any more: that true prayer is to be built up according to the law and principle of orderly arrangement; it is to be a cosmos for order, not a chaos for confusion. Prayer is a thought and implies a thinker; it implies intelligent design and bespeaks a designer. Behind acceptable and becoming supplication lies meditation: what do I want and what am I authorized to ask from God?

The so-called, Lord's Prayer, is mostly if not wholly drawn from that Old Testament which even Christ treated with such marked reverence or at least deference, and from which he quoted so constantly and so effectively. Indeed, the language of the Inspired Word constituted largely his dialect. Here we have rather a new combination and arrangement of expressions, already found in the Scriptures, than a wholly and radically new form of prayer. While the structure is original and novel, blocks from the Old Testament quarries may be easily recognized in the material of the building. It may therefore be interesting and instructive to compare its phraseology with the language of the then existing Scriptures, and note how nearly every petition here found is drawn from some previously recorded prayer, and how the whole of this prayer runs in the mould of a Scripture dialect. Perhaps this is the main lesson this prayer was meant to teach us—so to familiarize ourselves with Holy Scripture, that when we pray we shall naturally frame our supplications in inspired language.

We have taken some pains to trace the expressions of this prayer to their apparent Scriptural source or origin.

"Our Father." Isaiah 63. 16; 64. 8.

"Who art in Heaven." 2 Chronicles 20.6; Psalm 115. 3; Isaiah 58. 15, 59. 1.

"Hallowed be thy name." Leviticus 10. 3, 22. 32; 2 Samuel 7. 26; 1 Kings 8. 43; 1 Chronicles 17. 24; Nehemiah 9. 5; Psalm 52. 19, 111. 9; Isaiah 6. 3, 29. 23, 37. 20; Ezekiel 36. 23, 38. 23; Habakkuk 2. 14; Zechariah 14. 9; Malachi 1. 11, 4. 2.

"Thy kingdom come." Daniel 2. 44, 7. 13, 14, 27; Psalm 2. 6; Isaiah 2. 2-4, 9. 6-7; Jeremiah 23. 5; Zechariah 9. 9.

"Thy will be done." Psalm 40. 8; Ezra 7. 18; Dan. 4. 35; Psalm 143. 10. "On earth as it is in Heaven." Daniel 4. 35; Nehemiah 9. 6; Psalm 103. 19-22.

"Give us this day our daily Bread." Proverbs 30. 8; Exodus 16. 16; Job 23. 12; Psalm 34. 10; Isaiah 33. 16; Ezra 3. 4.

"And forgive us our debts." Exodus 34. 7; 1 Kings 8. 30-50; Psalm 32. 1, 103. 3-12, 130. 4; Daniel 9. 4-19; Jeremiah 31. 34, 36. 3.

"As we forgive our debtors." Nehemiah 5. 12, 13; Genesis 1. 17; 1 Samuel 25. 28, 29.

"And lead us not into temptation." Isaiah 3. 12, 9. 16; Proverbs 16. 29, 8. 20; Psalm 125. 5, 27. 11; Genesis 12. 1; Deut. 7. 2, 16; Proverbs 30. 8.

"But deliver us from evil." 1 Chron. 4. 10; Psalm 121. 7, 8; Jeremiah 15. 21; Psalm 56. 13.

"For Thine is the Kingdom." 1 Chron. 29. 2; Psalm 145. 13; Dan. 4. 34, 35.

"And the Power." 1 Chron. 29. 2.

"And the glory." 1 Chron. 29. 2; Daniel 7. 14.

"For ever and ever." Daniel 7. 18.

This prayer, which thus runs in the channel of Old Testament devoutness, is a model of brevity and comprehensiveness. It consists of,

1. An opening address in one short sentence: "Our Father who art in Heaven."

2. Three petitions, having main reference to God, His name, His Kingdom, His will; all of which the prayer would have as

universally revered, prevailing and controlling on Earth, as in Heaven.

3. Three, or possibly four, petitions, having main reference to man, the suppliant; that his daily needs may be met, his sins forgiven, his steps divinely guided, and his deliverance from all evil assured.

4. A final ascription to God, also three-fold, corresponding to the threefold petition addressed to Him in the first part of the prayer, and conceding heartily to Him the Kingdom, the Power and the Glory, which by right perpetually and inalienably belong to Him.

In all there are but nine short sentences, embracing but sixty-five words in the English, and in the Greek but fifty-seven; yet embracing every department of prayer. To those who can examine this prayer in the original Greek, many new beauties of poetic structure, parallelism and diction, hidden from the English reader, will become apparent.

Let us note also how comprehensive of all the elements that enter into prayer: Adoration.

Supplication for God's highest dues: worship and obedience.

"Our Father who art in Heaven," – Adoration.

Hallowed be Thy name. Thy Kingdom come, Thy will be done, etc. – Supplication for God's highest dues: worship and obedience.

Give us this day our bread – Supplication for man's daily need daily In all temporal things.

Forgive us our debts, And lead us, And deliver us, etc. – Supplication for man's highest good in spiritual things

For thine is the Kingdom etc. – Concluding ascription of worship

There is a deeper lesson taught in this so-called 'Lord's Prayer' than any that is implied in the use of this as a prescribed form. Notice our Lord's words: "After this manner." A manner is a flexible mould or matrix, not a fixed and uniform cast, which is to be filled out in every particular with a cast-iron uniformity. Among the most prevailing prayers ever offered it may be doubted whether any two ever were precisely alike. Of all those recorded in the Word of God, no two have any verbal resemblance which is at all exact, and even the two records of the Lord's Prayer which are given by Matthew and Luke show marked variations. Yet all inspired prayers have a certain conformity to one type, such as we see also amid all variations of species among *fauna* and *flora* in the natural world.

Does not our Lord mean to teach us that the highest model and mould for prayer is a scriptural one? Take, for instance, Jonah's prayer in the belly of the great fish, as recorded in Scripture (Jonah 2). As we follow this utterance of deep yearning toward God, when the prophet's soul fainted within him and he remembered the Lord, we find that the prayer is wholly composed of *passages of Scripture (Comp. Psalms 120. 1, 130. 1; Lam. 3. 55, 56; Ps. 1. 14, 23, 69. 1; Lam. 3 54; Isa. 38. 17; 2 Kings 17. 15; Ps. 31. 22; 1 Kings 8. 38, 39; I Sam. 12. 21; Ps. 18. 6; Ps. 61. 2, 34. 6, 88. 5-8; 42. 7.).* If carefully examined, and compared with other parts of the Old Testament, it will be found to be, not indeed a mere string of Scripture quotations or recitations, however appropriate, but a prayer which finds its expression in inspired language. Jonah was familiar with the book of the Law of the Lord, and was evidently wont to meditate therein. He had committed to his mind, if not to his memory, the words which the prophets before him had used in rebuking Israel; he remembered how Solomon prayed at the dedication of the temple; how Moses forewarned of the apostasies which led to the ruin of Jerusalem; how David and other sacred singers had called upon God in trouble and been delivered; and when out of the depths he cried unto the Lord, he naturally expressed his soul's penitence and petitions, in the language with which he was so familiar that his outpouring of soul naturally ran in these sacred channels. In a word, his prayer—unconsciously, it may be—took shape in a Scripture dialect, as in an inspired vernacular.

This is a suggestion which commends itself to a prayerful believer, not simply because it insures propriety and decorum in our approach to God, but for a reason even more important, namely, that a Scripture form of expression insures, or at least promotes, a scriptural frame of mind.

"We know not what we should pray for as we ought." There are three great lacks in prayer: The lack of proper words, of proper thoughts and desires, and of a proper spirit and motive. We are always in danger of asking what we are not warranted in asking. "This is the confidence that we have in Him, that, if we ask anything according to His will, He heareth us; and, if we know that He hear us, whatsoever we ask, we know that we have the petitions that we desired of Him." (I John 5. 13, 14).

How are we to attain this confidence? How may we know that what we ask is according to His will, and therefore within the range and scope of His own promise? We have only to model our prayers according to the manner of Scripture. A request, intelligently moulded in Scripture terms and on the basis of Scripture promises, is assuredly according to His will, and may be boldly urged at the throne of grace. Other prayers may not be improper or unscriptural, but we are in doubt until we have scriptural authority and warrant: then we get confidence to approach, and constancy to wait until the answer comes.

There is a principle here which is of vital importance. Of nothing does it need more to be said that of prayer: "See that thou make all things according to the pattern shewed to thee in the mount." (Hebrews 8. 5). Much of our sacred song, if examined in the light of Scripture, would be found to contain many sentiments unspiritual, misleading, and mischievous. And many a prayer is offered in private, aye, and in public, which has no warrant in the Word of God, which is the outbreathing of a worldly, unsanctified spirit, and not of the Spirit of God, and cannot be offered boldly, because faith has no promise to lay hold of, as of the horns of the altar.

For example, how can any suppliant confidently ask for riches, when there is no assurance beyond our daily bread? But how safe is the prayer that follows the Scripture model: "Give me neither poverty nor riches: feed me with food convenient for me." (Prov. 30. 8). How can we safely ask in any case that our own will may be accomplished, our own schemes may succeed, our own hopes be carried to fruition, when we may be selfishly planning for our own advancement or emolument, or at best be working in the energy of the flesh? But how bold we wax when we can lay all our work and will at His feet, and honestly say, "Thy will be done." The resort to a Scripture dialect acts as a constant corrective to carnality and selfishness and worldliness in prayer. The more we understand the teaching of Scripture, catch the meaning of its promises, penetrate beneath the letter to the spirit, and so enter into the mind of God, the more sure are we that our prayers are according to His will; and the more they will be according to His Word, which is the expression of His will.

Let any supplicating soul make trial of this test, and prove every petition by its conformity to the Scripture: and thereby may be revealed the reason why there has been so little boldness. But when one can plant his foot upon a distinct assurance of Scripture, a "thus saith the Lord"; or when the prayer is only the offering of a desire, authorized by distinct Scripture teaching, any other attitude but boldness is due to unbelief; whereas the suppliant who asks for what God has promised to give, or taught us to seek and authorized us to claim, becomes so daring that, like Jeremiah, jealous that God should not seem to dishonor His own word, he pleads:

"Do not disgrace the throne of Thy Glory!" (Jeremiah 14. 21)

In the lessons which immediately follow, as to the spirit of true prayer, the order is not always so obvious, or, perhaps, so important. But, for convenience and impressiveness of arrangement, we prefer to consider, first, three conditions of acceptable approach, which specially concern the inward state of the suppliant; and then, in a subsequent chapter, four of the higher secrets of prevailing power, which still concern the inward state of the praying man, but touch the deeper, higher mysteries of the great theme, and seem to form the natural apex and climax of these lessons.

The three conditions of acceptable approach have reference to a forgiving, a believing, and a persisting spirit in pleading with God.

IV. Forgiveness is a necessity, in the nature of things.

We come to God in prayer, first of all, to get forgiveness, for until that is gotten we can get nothing else, unless it be judgment. We are therefore taught that He can commune with us only from off and from over the mercy-seat.

In the gospel according to Matthew, the keynote is salvation: "Thou shalt call his name Jesus—Saviour—for he shall save his people from their sins." And, in the forefront of that gospel of salvation, we meet the great forerunner, that "Voice," whose stern message is, "Prepare ye the way of the Lord." There is a preparation for blessing, and we ourselves must make ready for it. There are crookedness's in our life which we must straighten out and rough nesses which we must make smooth, if we would have the King come to us, not as Adversary, to deliver the offender to the Judge to be condemned, and from the Judge to the officer to be cast into prison; but as himself Deliverer from prison, from condemnation, and from judgment. That preparation of the way of the Lord is found in confessing and forsaking of sin: so shall we find mercy. (Proverbs 28. 13; 1 John 1. 9) All unconfessed, unforsaken sin is a positive barrier between us and God.

We must therefore get our sins out of the way if we would approach unto God acceptably. That is our first need; and this can be done only by coming in penitence to the mercy-seat and presenting the Blood of Atonement, while, like the publican—who smote upon his breast, as though all sin were concentrated there, as in a stronghold of evil—we cry, " God, at the mercy-seat, meet me, the sinner!" (Luke 18. 13)

But, in order to open the heart to the reception of mercy, the exercise of mercy is necessary. To recognize a visible object there must be an organ of vision— not only something to be seen, but something to see with. Only love can understand love; only truth in the soul can recognize truth in the revelation; and so no man can come truly to a throne of grace, and appeal for forgiveness, while cherishing an unforgiving and vindictive spirit toward others. It takes grace to receive grace.

Imagine the high priest, venturing into the Holiest of All on the great Day of Atonement, bearing the blood of the slain victim as the warrant for his approach, and yet going into God's Presence cherishing hatred and revenge toward some fellow-sinner because of some trespass against himself! It is a contradiction that cannot be imagined. Bearing the blood which was the very sign and pledge of an innocent life given for his forfeited life, yet at the same moment bearing in his heart the guilty spirit of retaliation, which would exact full penalty for every sin or trespass committed against himself! The supposition bears the stamp of absurdity. Men cannot think such contradictions!

Here is the force of Shakespeare's delineation of Shylock. Shylock was a Jew, and so familiar from his birth with the idea of atonement. "Mercy rejoiceth against judgment" is written large over the whole levitical system of sacrifice.

Above all ether men, the Jew should be the last to exact penalty, and refuse mediation. Yet Shylock rejects all ransom and will have his pound of flesh. The myriad-minded dramatist makes the character of the exorbitant and merciless usurer all the more hideous, because he who was so early taught to pray for mercy, knew nothing of rendering the deeds of mercy.

And so our Lord, in that parable of the two debtors, (Matt, 18. 21-35). shows us the impossibility of receiving, if we do not impart, forgiveness. Even the formal declaration of forgiveness which followed the confession of debt and bankruptcy, was cancelled and revoked, when he, who had been forgiven the immense debt of ten thousand talents, took by the throat his fellow-servant who owed him one hundred pence, and mercilessly cast him into prison despite his entreaties! The greater debtor had been utterly bankrupt and yet had found compassion and release; but he would not exercise like compassion toward one whose debt was so small that payment would follow patience. In him there was neither the grace of pity nor of patience: and he who after forgiveness was too hard-hearted to forgive, showed himself incapable of really receiving or even recognizing forgiveness. His last deed of cruelty toward a fellow- servant involved another deed of outrage toward their common master, and he who had been pronounced forgiven was now hopelessly delivered to the tormentors.

V. The next lesson is one on believing: "Have faith in God."

This is a deeper lesson than any superficial glance can read. We are taught that "he that cometh to God must believe that He is and is a rewarder of them that diligently seek Him." But a careful search into our Lord's words, in this fifth lesson, reveals mysteries which like those of his parables evade the careless eye.

Comparing the passages in Matthew, Mark, and Luke (Matthew 17. 20, 21, Mark 11. 22-24; Luke 17. 5, 6.), we find that, while all of them are essentially lessons on faith, they have both marked resemblances and differences. Both Matthew and Luke compare the principle of faith to "a grain of mustard-seed," but the application of faith is in one case to the removal of "this mountain," and in the other case to the withering of the fig-tree and the plucking up of the sycamine tree. As such similarities or dissimilarities cannot be without design, let us, if we would pierce to the secret chamber of this teaching, examine closely.

Obviously there can be no access, or even approach, to God, in the holiest place, without the believing spirit. The

Presence that fills the secret place is not a presence revealed to the bodily eye. Faith is the soul's organ of vision, hearing, feeling, whereby we behold, hear and 'handle' God. Hence the reality and power of all communion with Him must hang on this: how far His own word of promise is believed. To come into the closet, believing He is there, and ready to impart Himself to the suppliant, is to get answer before we call and find Him hearing while yet we are speaking. Our Lord therefore says, "Have faith in God literally, Have the faith of God. So essential to prevailing, effective supplication is this element, that it is fundamental—as though God had said. Between you and Me there can be no contact or communication, until you believe in Me, My existence, My readiness to reward your diligent seeking.' If the basis of all friendship among men is mutual trust— confidence in one another, so that I may properly say to a professed friend, 'if you cannot believe me and believe in me, there can be no communion between us,' how can we expect any friendly relations with God so long as we deny or doubt His existence, or question or impugn His word of assurance? The lesson taught by our Lord on faith in prayer takes this primitive principle or law for granted and builds upon it. But his teaching advances far beyond this self-evident truth.

His comparison of faith to "a grain of mustard-seed" must not be dismissed as though it had reference only to the littleness of our faith. He does not set a premium on littleness. He commended the poor widow who cast in her two mites into the treasury, but not because they were mites, but because they were her all. The mustard-seed is small, but it is the hiding of God's power. It represents the omnipotence of Life. The mountain is but a mass of dead inert matter. It cannot, with all its massiveness, move itself, for it does not represent any power but that of resistance. All force or energy is vital—it is linked with life. The mustard-seed, though it be least of seeds sown in the soil, represents the principle of life, and therefore of growth, expansion, reproduction. Let the little mustard-seed drop into the crevices of the rock and it can split the solid mass and heave it from its bed, by simple growth.

Faith is mighty, not because it is small, but because it is the hiding of God's power. It is the seed of God—having in it God's life, and where it lodges there is growth, motion, expansion, reproduction: so far as it is genuine and God-like—the faith of God—it exercises the Power of God and is irresistible.

We notice however a marked dissimilarity in the application of faith. Why is it one case the mountain and in the other the sycamine tree?

The mountain suggests a massive obstacle—something to be surmounted with difficulty, to be removed with still greater difficulty, but which lies in the way of advance. The sycamine tree may be comparatively small, but is peculiar for its deep and fast-clinging roots, that take hold on the soil and defy uprooting—and this naturally suggests inward difficulties, as the mountain does outward obstacles. Faith is equal to both.

A careful examination of the context of each passage may suggest a true exegesis. It is Matthew who makes Christ refer to the mountain—and it is he who suggests the outward hindrance. Christ had just come down from the mountain where he had been transfigured, and he met a man whose son was possessed of a demon whom the disciples had proved unable to cast out. The Devil was heaping mountain upon mountain to obstruct the progress of the kingdom; and because of their unbelief they could neither surmount nor remove these mountains, and they had to fall back on the power of Christ. Once more He teaches them that all depends on their faith. Unbelief makes them powerless; faith, irresistible.

On the other hand, in Luke, we meet the sycaminetree, which however small has a tenacious hold upon the earth, suggesting not so much a formidable obstacle to advance, as a deep-rooted inward sin, habit, lust or passion—a disposition ineradicable by unaided human power and self-will, and needing divine transforming energy. Our common language embodies this thought when we speak of "deeply-rooted habits and customs," and of prejudices and passions, "hard to eradicate," etc.

This seems to be the exact thought of the Lord himself in the passage cited from Luke. Examining the context we find Christ teaching a lesson on forgiveness, that it should be so long-suffering in patience and so habitual in exercise that if, in one day, an offence should be seven times repeated and seven times repented of, our forgiveness toward the offender must survive such a trial, and our gracious temper be unwearied in its forbearance. Nay, not until seven times, but until seventy times seven, must such repetition of forgiving love be equal. And it was in view of such prospective demand on love's magnanimity that, as with one voice, the apostles exclaimed, "Lord, increase our faith!" as though only such increase of faith could make possible such rich outlays of forbearing compassion and undiscouraged hope. Such demands are daily made, or at least liable to be made, upon, the working machinery of our daily life in contact with our fellow-men, that nothing short of closer fellowship with God can supply adequate motive power to keep that machinery running; or, as the beloved Arnot used to say, when the pebble gets between the millstones, the miller lets in more head of water, to grind it to powder.

That, however, which is most marked in this lesson on Faith is the Authority conceded to faith and with which faith is clothed.

In this the three evangelists agree. Matthew's record reads: "If ye have faith, ye shall say to this mountain, Remove hence to yonder place, and it shall remove." Mark says: "Whosoever shall say unto this mountain, BE thou removed, and be thou cast into the sea; and shall not doubt... he shall have whatsoever he saith." Luke says: "If ye had faith... ye might say unto this sycamine tree, BE thou plucked up, and be thou planted in the sea, and it should obey you."

The coincidence is too remarkable to be either accidental or unimportant. In all these cases it is not "pray " but " say," not the word of petition but of direction, not as of a suppliant but as of a sovereign.

This we regard as the central, vital heart of this great lesson on Faith. The Master of all girds the servant with His own power and intrusts him with authority to command. Faith claims not only blessing but power to bless. This lesson is at first sight so astounding as to seem incredible—it passes all understanding, and faith itself staggers at such promises.

Let us reverently seek to take in the marvelous thought. Faith in God so unites to God that it passes beyond the privilege of asking to the power of commanding. This language of Christ is not that of a request, however bold, but of a FIAT. God said, "BE LIGHT! AND LIGHT WAS! " (Gen. 1. 3 (Hebrew)). Such is the sublime announcement in Genesis. And He says to His disciples,

"Concerning the work of My hands,

Command ye Me!" (Isaiah 45. 11).

And so—marvelous fact! the child of God, laying hold by faith of the Power of the Omnipotent One, issues his fiat: "Be thou removed!" "Be thou plucked up by the roots!" and it is so.

Can we find any illustration or interpretation of this philosophy of prayer in the Economy of Nature? In the universe of matter there are so-called 'Universal Forces,' such as Light and Heat, Gravity and Chemical Affinity, Attraction and Repulsion, Adhesion and Cohesion, Magnetism and Electricity. They all work within certain well-defined lines and limits which are called "Laws," or 'modes of operation.' Man has only to understand and conform to those laws or conditions, and act in accordance with these 'modes of Force' or Energy, and he may actually command them to do his bidding. We are only beginning after the lapse of sixty centuries to understand the grandeur of those words, *"Let them have dominion."* (Gen. 1. 26)

Omnipotent as are the powers of nature, this is still true:

OBEY THE LAW OF THE POWER,

AND THE POWER OBEYS YOU.

To apply this principle is to see this truth. Obey the laws of Light, and Light becomes your Artist, delineating with matchless accuracy and beauty every line and lineament of a beloved face or natural landscape. Obey the laws of Heat, and it becomes your Great Assayer, refining and purifying your metals; your giant Manufacturer, making them ready to receive any impression or take any shape at your will. Obey the laws of Gravity, and it comes at your summons with Titanic hammer to beat the rocks to powder, pound the slag out of huge lumps of iron, and like a Master Mechanic mould the most stubborn material for useful ends. We obey likewise the laws of Magnetism, and it becomes our Pilot to guide our vessels upon unknown seas, or a valuable Therapeutic to restore health to diseased frames. We obey the laws of Electricity, and it becomes our Messenger, Motor, Illuminator, all at once!

In the Spiritual Realm there is one all- subduing, all-controlling Force, Power or Energy: The Holy Spirit of God. It is not too much to say that God gives His Holy Spirit "*to them that obey Him*" (Acts 5. 32) and that we have only to regard and observe those laws and limits within which the Spirit acts, and we find even His blessed power placed at our disposal: in other words, it is still divinely true: Obey the Law of the Power and the Power obeys you.

Conform to the Laws and modes of the Spirit's operations, and in the work of God's hands you may command the Spirit's Power. It was a glimpse of this truth that led Coleridge to write the famous couplet:

"Faith is an affirmation and an act,

That bids eternal truth be fact."

To which we venture to add, in expansion of the divine thought:

Faith issues its sublime decree,

Its holy fiat: LET IT BE!

Commands the deeply-rooted tree,

Be plucked up! planted in the sea!

Or bids the mountain to depart,

Believing, doubting not in heart,

That what Faith willeth shall be done,

Because Faith's will with God's is one,

By mystic union with His Son.

Concerning work of God's own hand,

He bids us His own power command.

And so prayer asks not, but decrees,

Knows no impossibilities.

VI. In this group of lessons, one remains, which indicates another condition of prevailing prayer, and acceptable approach to God, namely, persistence in pleading, or as our Lord phrases it, "Men ought always to pray and not to faint!"

This lesson of importunity is taught under the striking imagery of a double parable: 'The Unjust Judge,' and the 'Friend in Need.'

The former is a parable of contrasts. The widow had no advocate to plead her cause: her husband, who was her natural protector and defender, being dead, she had no man to appear in court in her behalf, and so was compelled to present herself and urge her own plea. The judge was a man who had neither piety nor philanthropy: "he feared not God nor regarded man hence there was no moral or religious principle in him to appeal to, not even human affection and humane sympathy. To him the widow was a mere beggar, suing for a favor: to her person and to her plea he was alike indifferent, and like Gallio "cared for none of these things" which on principles of essential justice and humanity should move any judge to action. Yet, as a beggar and because she was a beggar, he wished to be rid of her, and there was only one way: to do as she wanted. She would not be silenced. Matters could not be settled, till they were settled right. His selfishness was the only tender point in his character— and that she touched, and it responded. He granted her request because in no other way he could silence her or dismiss her.

At every point a contrast is either expressed or implied. The Infinitely Just Judge, the Infinitely Good God—who has an eternal regard for inherent righteousness and rectitude, and an infinite love for mankind, together with a holy indignation against all injustice and oppression, robbery of the poor and unfairness of dealing toward the helpless and friendless—is contrasted with this human judge. God's unspeakable love toward His own elect, and divine jealousy for their vindication, are in contrast to the indifference and utter selfishness of this earthly magistrate toward this widow. The presence of the Great Advocate at Court— Jesus Christ, the Righteous, God's own Beloved Son, and the Last Adam, our Brother in the flesh—is in contrast to the absence of any friend or defender to espouse her cause and conduct her suit.

Moreover the argument is cumulative. For, if the widow prevailed over such indifference simply by her importunity, and thus, without any advocate, wrested justice from such a judge, when there was left only abominable selfishness of the lowest sort to appeal to— how much more shall the believer prevail, when he meets, in the Celestial Court, Everlasting Love as well as Infinite Equity, seated on the Bench of Judgment, and when he has an all-powerful Advocate, and also finds arrayed in advance on his own side all the perfections of the Godhead in the person of the Judge!

The other part of this twin parable teaches the same general lesson in a form perhaps even more impressive. The neighbor, to whom the appeal for the three loaves is addressed, is a friend, and can as such be appealed to; but he also is selfish, though neither destitute of philanthropy nor of humanity. He is in bed with his children: it is midnight, and perhaps damp and chilly as well as dark. He would gladly be rid of the necessity of getting up, striking a light, and finding the three loaves whose loan is asked by the other. He, like the unjust judge, finally yields to the demand of his neighbor, but in supplying the need he is not primarily moved by either friendship or sympathy; but, because he wants to be let alone and to have the quiet of his rest and sleep unbroken, he rises and gives the suppliant as many as he needeth. Selfishness dictates regard for his comfort, and comfort there can be none, while that knocking and calling goes on at the gate!

How simple and forcible the lesson, and how convincing the indirect argument! How much more will your Heavenly Father give bread, as much as is needed, when they are His own needy children who stand knocking at His gate; and when Paternal Love, unselfish and self-sacrificing and self-forgetting, rules absolutely in His heart! Nay, when it is His own unchanging Word of Promise, His challenge to "ask," "seek," "knock," which brings us as suppliants to our Father's House where there is enough and to spare; and on the very gate of which is written, "Knock and it shall be opened unto you!"

Thus, in both forms of parable, one great lesson appears, garmented in a slightly different attire: Faint not, but continue in prayer. If the vision tarry wait for it, as the High Priest, entering the Holiest of All, in the prescribed way, if he had there found no Shekinah fire burning, and had neither beheld any divine vision nor heard any divine voice responding, would have had but one course to pursue—to wait until the cloud of glory filled the House, and the divine communication was given.

In the gospel according to Luke, (Luke 11. 9-13). the verses which follow this latter parable have a connection that is vital and essential. There is every mark of intentional continuity. "And I say unto you, ask, and it shall be given you; seek, and ye shall find; knock, and it shall be opened unto you." Notice the "and" which so closely links what follows with what precedes as to forbid any pause in the discourse; and note also the advance in thought: "Ask"—the formal request; "Seek"—the inward and intense quest of what is asked; "Knock"—the repeated and unwearied asking and seeking, for whoever knocks but once?

There is possibly a hint in this second parable as to requests offered for others, as in the former the widow was asking somewhat for herself. What a lesson on missions is here taught us. It is the midnight' hour with the vast multitudes of our race, and their needs come to us with the appeal of an awful destitution, like messengers from afar appealing for hospitality. We have not the means to meet the emergency and supply the spiritual destitution of the thousand millions of the race. But God is nigh, and He has abundance. He can thrust laborers forth into the harvest field, and move His own saints to pour out their treasures to maintain the workmen and the work. Above all, He can bestow the Holy Spirit in answer to prayer, and that means Bread of Life to famishing peoples. O for the importunity of Faith to ask with boldness, undiscouraged perseverance, and confident assurance!

The history of believers gloriously illustrates the power of importunity in prayer. We select one.

George Gillespie, of Edinburgh, will be remembered as the devout and gifted man who, being requested, by the moderator of the famous 'Westminster Assembly,' to ask special aid as to the definition of God in the Catechism which the Westminster divines were preparing, began his prayer as follows:

"O God, who art a Spirit, infinite, eternal and unchangeable in thy Being, Power, Wisdom, Holiness, Justice, Goodness and Truth" — And that opening sentence was at once adopted as an inspired answer to the question, "What is God?"

This same Gillespie, when, afterward, the nature and constitution of the Christian church came up for consideration, rendered another service scarce less distinguished. Great anxiety was felt on account of John Selden, leader of the Erastian party, and the most learned man in England, especially rich in Rabbinical lore, and a master of the arts of logic and rhetoric. His argument was so sophistical and yet apparently unanswerable, that when he concluded the cause seemed lost. But Gillespie calmly arose, took up Selden's Erastian positions, and exposing their fallacy and sophistry, tore his argument to shreds.

On the fragment of paper whereon he had apparently been making notes, was found a short prayer in Latin, written again and again from top to bottom of the page: "Da lucem, Domine" (Give light, O Lord!"). While the master sophist had been weaving the web of his argument, Gillespie had been knocking importunately at Heaven's gate for power to see and expose its false reasoning.

CHAPTER III. THE HIGHER SECRETS OF PRAYER.

We are reaching toward a climax. One remaining group of four lessons remains, which seems to belong further on in this course of study, as pertaining to the higher classes in the school of Christ, for these lessons appear to touch the inmost heart of the theme—the 'esoteric' secrets of prevailing power in supplication and intercession, such as the filial spirit in our approach to God, the self-abasement which comes from a deep sense of sin and ill-desert, the agreement of sympathetic souls in joint supplication, and the identity of praying saints with the Great Intercessor Himself.

All these lessons, with those three of the preceding group, are related so closely that it is neither easy to separate them, nor to determine their precise order. For instance, in the case of the two lessons on faith and on the filial spirit, one merges, almost melts, into the other; yet obviously a son's faith in his Father is something in advance of a suppliant's faith in a promising God, where the sense of son ship does not displace the sense of mere servantship and servile subjection. And, as to the exact order, it is not essential that we shall either discover or follow it: all we can do is to look for the inherent indications of orderly arrangement. Thus we have felt that the forgiving spirit belongs first as the primary condition of asking for that first of all gifts—pardon; and that simple faith in God as a reality and verity is the next condition of all approach to a personal Helper, and that this again prepares us for the persistent pleading in which if there be not 'faith' there must be 'fainting.'

We are confirmed in this conviction that the four lessons now grouped together, have a peculiarly close relation, as all belonging to the New Testament revelations of Prayer as we shall see; whereas those just considered are Old Testament lessons, however enforced by the new and higher unveilings of truth. Abraham and Moses, David and Daniel, Elijah and Elisha, all knew the doctrine of forgiveness, of faith, and of persistence. Moses and Elijah, as prominently as any New Testament saints, exemplified them all. But the idea of the believer's son ship, of a personal mercy-seat, of a symphony of prayer produced by the Holy Spirit, and of supplication founded upon identification with the Son of God—all these are revelations that waited for the Incarnation, Resurrection and Ascension of our Lord.

VII. If, in the present group, any one lesson belongs at the front, it is the Lord's teaching about the Filial spirit, which in Luke immediately and inseparably follows that on importunity.

It is obvious that such confidence as is begotten of conscious son ship in God's family, belongs much farther on in attainment and in the secrets of prevalence, than the general faith in God as God, which any suppliant may feel who has not yet learned that he may call God "Father" in a new and redemptive sense. And so, if we mistake not, a progress of doctrine runs through all this teaching and makes it progressive.

This lesson on *Filial Confidence* (Matthew 7. 7-1 1; Luke 11. 11-13.) is thus a higher lesson on faith—the faith which the child and son reposes in the Father. The God whom we meet in the Holiest of All is Our Father who art in Heaven." To the Hebrews of old He was The Almighty, Jehovah, the God of Power, the Creator, Ruler, Judge; God of the Covenant; but how seldom do we meet in the Old Testament any reference to Him as Father. Those of the olden time could not yet apprehend this aspect of God: they had not conceived the coming Messiah as the 'Last Adam,' 'First Born among many brethren,' and hence holding with man fraternal relations. Hence they were not prepared to understand, as we are, the Paternal relation of God the Father to us who are sons and heirs of God in Christ Jesus. This is the reason why the Fatherhood of God in Christ is the great truth of the New Testament, and how it is that one short phrase, in Christ is the key that unlocks the whole New Covenant with all its mysteries. Every book in the New Testament is explained by it. In Romans, Justified in Christ; Galatians, Sanctified in Christ; Philippians, Satisfied in Christ; Ephesians, in Christ, one; in Colossians, in Christ, complete, etc.

Our Lord teaches us two things about the Fatherhood of God, which are to be our constant encouragement and inspiration in prayer: first, He "knoweth how to give good gifts to His children and, secondly, He wills to give even "His Holy Spirit to them that ask Him." He has infinite wisdom and knowledge to guide His choice of gifts, and infinite goodness and love to prompt Him to the bestowal of them. Paul, in that climax on Prayer in Ephesians, presents the same double argument from Love and Power (Ephes. 3. 17-21). Power assures us He is able; Love assures us He is willing. Without Power He might be willing, but unable; without Love He would be able, but unwilling. The child of God who has the sense of son ship comes boldly to One who is both able and willing.

Let us tarry to notice our Lord's illustrations of the Divine Fatherhood. "If a son shall ask bread of any of you that is a father, will he give him a stone? or if he ask a fish, will he for a fish give him a serpent? or if he ask an egg, will he offer him a scorpion?" Here is a threefold contrast: between bread, the staff of life, and the stone which the Jew thought of as dead, and as used to kill and slay the blasphemer and disobedient, and which was, therefore, the symbol of death; between the fish, a form of animal food, and the serpent, the symbol of the Devil, who destroys instead of nourishing; and between the egg, which has the germ of reproduction, and the scorpion, whose sting is painful and often fatal. It is not necessary to suppose that our Lord here imagines a human father as malignantly mocking a child's request by an intentional substitution of what is useless and even harmful for what is needful and helpful. He may mean no more than this, that even the most ignorant parent knows better what a son needs and means to ask for, than to substitute such gifts for those which are sought.

But, however we interpret details, the lesson is plain: we may trust God's wisdom to make no mistake in the conferring of what we need, and His love not to make the worse mistake of withholding what is in His power to bestow. If we ask Him for the Bread of Life, we never get the stone of death; if, for the food that up builds strength, we never get the virus and venom that destroys health; if, for the nourishing egg we shall not get the stinging scorpion.

To some who are prone to symbolism, these words mean three classes of gifts, and represent the Trinity. The Bread of Life stands for the common mercies from the Father's hands; the Son is represented by the Fish, which was to the early disciples the great symbol of Jesus, Son of God, Saviour of men; and the Spirit, the source of all spiritual life and regeneration, by the Egg.

We are content, however, to draw simply the broad general lesson of filial confidence—the assurance which the spirit of the son engenders, that our Father in Heaven both knows how to give good gifts to them that ask Him, and is more willing than are earthly parents, to bestow on His suppliant child all that he asks or needs; aye, and better than all, that

He knows how to withhold, when to with-hold is the wiser course and the better way of giving. For we know not what we should pray for as we ought. We make the mistake of asking for the stone when we think it to be bread; or for what would prove a venomous curse or a stinging disappointment, if we had it. And so filial confidence trusts Him to keep back what would be consumed on our selfish lusts, or prove to our damage, and to give us instead what feeds true spiritual life, instead of granting us our request and sending leanness to our soul.

VIII. The lesson of humility and self-abasement may seem at first sight to belong among the earliest to be taught and learned; yet as a matter of fact this lesson demands much previous Christian attainment, and cannot be understood without much spiritual maturity.

Our Lord teaches self-abasement in prayer by a most dramatic and striking contrast of a self-complacent pharisee and a penitent and contrite publican. These two men went up into the Temple Courts to pray. The pharisee stood and thus "prayed with himself"—a happy phrase to describe what was more a soliloquy than a supplication: "God, I thank thee that I am not as other men are; extortioners, unjust, adulterers—or even as this publican. I fast twice in the week; I give tithes of all that I possess." Thirty-four words in the English, and five times the capital "I" is found in these three short sentences! There is not a word of adoration, confession, or supplication here: it is all self-granulation, under the presence or pretext of thanksgiving. The Greek is still stronger than the English rendering, "God I thank thee that I am not as the rest of men." Perhaps it was all true that he was not: there is not a hint here that he was lying. He may have been all that he affirmed—neither 'rapacious,' nor 'unrighteous,' nor 'adulterous'—a man of clean outward life, and much above the publican, the despised tax-man, on whom he loftily looked down. But is very plain that he was puffed up with pride. He reminds one of the 'selfmade' men who strut about with the pride of the peacock, if not the vanity of the turkey-gobbler, and boast of what they have become and have achieved—all 'by themselves'! The pharisee, at least in the presence of a holy God, might have taken a low place. In the light of the Shekinah his 'comeliness' should have lost its beauty in his eyes and have been 'turned into corruption.' But he was blinded and dazzled, not by the glory of God, but by his own superior excellence. The fact is that he did not get into the

Holy of Holies at all, nor come near to the mercy-seat. He was in the outermost court, and knew nothing of drawing nigh unto God, for none can approach truly into that inmost Presence without a new insight into his own innate, inward corruption, as in the glare of the midday sun nothing seems clean.

The publican may have been all that the pharisee thanked God he was not. Taxcollecting was in Jewish eyes the brand of ignominy and villainy. To lend oneself to a foreign and oppressive power as a tool of tyranny, to wrest from a poor and conquered province a tribute which represented no equivalent of good received or blessing enjoyed, was to the Jew of that day the supreme sign of a mean and dastardly nature. The 'publican' and 'the harlot' were linked in the very speech of that day, because both made a sale of virtue to the highest bidder and lent themselves body and soul to vice.

Publicans, having forfeited all claim to respect, usually came to deserve none.

Their opportunity for extortion was ample, and they generally improved it. The collecting of taxes was "farmed out." A chief among the publicans, like Zaccheus, would have a large district under control and let out the job to subordinates, who mercilessly took what they chose, paid the government what it demanded and levied, and kept the rest; and, as the Roman authorities cared little for the complaints of an oppressed province, there was no remedy. The people were ground as between millstones, but had to submit.

Zaccheus, when salvation came to his house, that day of grace, said, "If I have taken anything from any man by false accusation, I restore fourfold." The 'false accusation,' referred to, was the levying of a tax greater than the government authorized, a false impost, and for personal gain; the chance for extortion was immense, and how unjust such extortion often was may be gathered from the 'fourfold' restoration which was proposed in order to cover it. Moreover, as publicans and harlots were ranked together and alike despised, it was but natural that they should often consort together. Neither of them had any 'character' to maintain or any 'reputation' to lose in the public eyes; and as the publican had plenty of money which came easily, and the outcast woman had 'virtue' for sale and the price was cheap, it was inevitable that the two classes should deserve the association which they had in common parlance.

But, whatever the guilt of the publican, the redeeming feature is that he knew and felt it. Nominally he stood 'afar off'; really he was much the nearer of the two, to the Divine Presence. Remembering the words of the Psalm,

"Mine iniquities have taken hold upon me,

So that I am not able to look up;

They are more than the hairs of mine head,

Therefore my heart faileth me"; (Psalm 40. 12)

he could not so much as lift up his eyes toward Heaven, and, as though all the possibilities of sin were hidden within him, he smote upon his own breast and could find courage but for one sentence: "God meet, at the mercy-seat, me, the Sinner!" (Psalm 40. 12.) It is remarkable that, even in this one sentence of six words in the Greek, there is conveyed adoration, confession, and supplication; and that the expression, "me the sinner," implies a sense of pre-eminence in sin, while the one word translated 'merciful' is the verb exactly corresponding to the noun, 'mercy-seat.'

When the High Priest went into the Holiest of All with blood of atonement, it was in garments of humiliation. We cannot think of him as entering that secret chamber of God's Presence with any proud confidence in his own righteousness. On the contrary, everything combined to produce overwhelming conviction and consciousness of sin. He went within the veil in the capacity of a representative Sin-Bearer. The only day in which he dared to go in at all was the great Day of Atonement; the only way in which he dared to go, even then, was with the blood of a vicarious victim. That day was the day of confession, both of his own sins and the sins and errors of the whole people. The slain goat and the goat 'Azazel' told of guilt that must both be expiated by a forfeited life, and removed from before the face of Him who is of 'purer eyes than to behold evil,' and cannot 'look upon iniquity.' Thus everything about the Day of Atonement spoke of sin—of damning, separating guilt—confessed, forsaken, forgiven, renounced, removed; and there was but one attitude of soul which would not have been a mockery: namely, a bowing down in contrition and penitence.

Who can think of the High Priest as passing within the veil, and there, facing the searching glory of the Infinite One, uttering the pharisees self-complacent soliloquy! Was not the whole scene, enacted on the great Day of Atonement, one long-drawn-out publican's prayer?

We cannot but feel, however, that this overwhelming sense of sin, which leads to such self-abasement and abandonment of all self-trust, belongs among the higher secrets of power in prayer. Conviction of sin, deep, abiding and prostrating, is not only very rare, but it indicates and indexes a peculiar ripeness of Christian character. The holiest saints have always been the most profoundly convicted sinners. The nearer we get to God by grace the more we feel our distance by nature.

It requires a trained eye to see minute defects and detect slight blemishes. A painting that a common, undisciplined observer thinks a superb work of art, the educated artist condemns perhaps as a worthless daub, not because he is hypercritical, but because he has a higher and truer conception of accuracy in drawing, propriety in grouping, skill in coloring. Michel Angelo had so studied Anatomy that he could detect the least error in the proportions of the human form when delineated on canvas, and had so studied Nature's moods and combinations that he instinctively knew when a painting violated her canons of truth and taste. And so it does not follow, because I seem to myself far more a sinner than I did when first I found Jesus, that I am worse; it may be I am far more like God, only I have learned to detect sin where once I saw none: the painting has become the daub, not because there is any change in the painting, but because there is a change in the eye that scans it. The pharisee looked at himself and saw nothing to condemn, but much to applaud: the publican, looking at himself, saw nothing to approve, but everything to condemn and abhor. However great the difference in the two characters, the greater difference was in the eyes that looked upon them: in one case blinded by self-righteous pride; in the other opened to behold the hatefulness and sinfulness of sin.

Be not surprised, therefore, child of God, if, as you seek to draw nigh to God and to be like God, your sense of sin becomes more intolerable. Thank God if you see clearly only do not stop with a sight of self: 'look away to Jesus the author and perfecter of your faith'; and knowing yourself, ask that you may know Himself, and lose even the sense and sight of your sin in the sense and sight of your Saviour. Then alone does conviction and contrition reach its perfect work— in fixing your gaze upon the Great Sin-Bearer!

Before we leave this dramatic contrast of the pharisee and publican, let us learn how different are God's judgments of character from those of men. The pharisee justified himself but God condemned him; the publican condemned himself but God justified him. Society is an inclined plane—at the top stands the pharisee, outwardly correct and moral, and even punctilious about prayers, fasting's, tithing's; at the bottom stands the publican, guilty of sins of extortion, injustice, impurity; but, in God's eyes, the proud pharisee is going down and the penitent publican is going up, and they will pass each other on the way, and exchange places in the coming kingdom; for,

"He that exalteth himself shall be abased,

And he that humbleth himself shall be exalted."

IX. We come now to a lesson on Agreement in Prayer, the first and only one which appears to be directed toward joint supplication. It is perhaps not so much a new lesson, as a new application of principles already conveyed to us in this teaching of the secrets of prevailing supplication.

The key-word of this lesson is Agreement, but the original word is a stronger one than can be represented by the word "agree." It means to symphonize. The term is itself a whole revelation. Symphony is a musical term, and refers not to an accidental or arbitrary agreement of notes in the musical scale, but to an eternal and unchangeable law—the law of the chord. Harmony is determined by the interval between notes. No symphony of sounds is possible where notes are not in accord with the instrument generally, tuned up to the proper pitch, and where they are not correspondent with each other in the musical scale. A careless touch upon an instrument often evokes not harmony but the worst of discords. It takes the intelligent, discriminating touch of the musician to evoke a symphony, for he instinctively strikes keys which are accordant.

The symphony of prayer, in which believing suppliants unite, is not the result of any mere formal agreement or covenant with each other, proper as this may often be, as in the case of Daniel and his companions. (Daniel 2. 17-19.) Such agreement is only effective when it is the result of the Holy Spirit's own working, He bringing disciples into accord first with Himself and then with each other, like a master musician who first tunes all the keys according to a concert pitch, and then strikes such notes as are prepared to blend harmoniously in one chord.

The word, symphonize is a trope—and suggests the entire body of true suppliants as the key-board of a vast musical instrument, which is in tune with the mind and purpose of God. The Holy Spirit, the divine musician, lays his hand, like a true artist, on two or more keys, which He has first brought into harmonious relations with God's will and each other, and which are thus prepared to sound in the divine ear a perfect chord; and so there come into the ear of God both melody and harmony,—the melody of acceptable individual prayer; the harmony of acceptable joint supplication.

The implied inference is that you and I cannot arbitrarily "agree" as touching anything that we shall ask, and then plead this promise. Except so far as we first agree with the Holy Spirit, so that our prayer becomes the expression of the divine will, there can be no such agreement with each other as this promise implies. In other words, sympathy with God must be the basis of symphony among disciples. When the Holy Spirit is thus able to move upon hearts of disciples, however far separated by distance but still united by spiritual proximity and sympathy, He often touches suppliants who are strangers to each other and brings them into unconscious accord and concord in prayer for the same objects. Thus, when the secret thoughts of many hearts are revealed, we shall undoubtedly find that praying disciples, far apart, in distant lands, often unknown to each other, have been led of the Spirit into simultaneous and sympathetic prayer for the same blessings, praying at the same time for the same things, with a degree of holy accord, explainable only by the fact that the same divine Spirit has been moving in their hearts and interceding in and through them.

What boundless paths and fields of suggestion this lesson on symphony in prayer opens up! yes, and what possible power too. What an illuminating light is thrown on our Lord's words about joint prayer for the harvest-held, and that divine thrusting forth of laborers (Matt. 9. 37, 38.) into its wide, vast vacancies, which is the one sovereign remedy for the world's need, and the efficacy of which is so illustrated in the thrusting forth of Barnabas and Saul from the praying assembly at Antioch! (Comp. Acts 13. 1-5.)

Abundant examples might be supplied of the power of prayer that is offered in accordance with such teachings.

Early in the last century, about 1729, a great movement began at Oxford under the Wesley brothers, George Whitefield, and that other little group of four or five, who covenanted together to join each other in the pursuit of personal holiness, and sought to learn the secrets of spiritual power in service. It was not the first time God has chosen a few to teach the many, and in a brief period to leave on record a lesson for all ages. At the end of six years these 'Methodists' numbered but sixteen. But on this little band came the Spirit of God in such power that, through their preaching, prayers, and testimony, the whole Church of Christ was lifted to a higher level. It may be doubted whether, since Christ ascended, any equal number of believers have in such a way wrought more powerfully upon the history and destiny of men. The condition of society, both within and without the pale of the visible Church, was so deplorable that Evangelical faith had scarcely a name to live. Deism was preached in Christian pulpits, and libertinism was practiced in social life with unblushing audacity. Infidelity and irreligion seemed to be sweeping before them the last remnants of a pure Christian doctrine and practice. Missions had almost ceased to be even the admitted duty of the Church, and formalism of the most stereotyped and petrified type seemed to be encasing the Church in its heartless shell of rites and ceremonies.

The results of those little conferences and prayer meetings, held in Oxford, can never be known until the Books are opened. We trace them immediately in the brilliant career of Whitefield, and a score of other Evangelists, and in the open-air services, which, for vastness of congregations, magnitude of results, and permanent revolution of society, can be compared to nothing since apostolic days; in the rapid creation of the most aggressive denomination of Christians, now numbering millions; and in the amazing multiplication of praying circles in all parts of the world, the revival of Evangelical doctrine and piety, and the birth of the new era of missions. Ten years later, in 1739, the first Methodist Society was formed. Twenty years later, 1749, Jonathan Edwards was stirring all New England by his preaching, and sending forth his trumpet-call to universal prayer for the effusion of the Spirit. Sixty years later, 1789, William Carey was poring over the question of a world's evangelization, and organizing a world-wide campaign. It seems incredible, but the present state of Evangelical faith and Evangelistic activity may be traced directly back to those meetings which began in 1729, in the hearts of less than a dozen men who yearned to know God and serve Him completely, and were by the Spirit brought so into accord with God and each other that their prayers symphonized.

X. The last lesson lifts us to the grand climax: We are bidden to ask IN THE NAME OF CHRIST.

This lesson, which is obviously last in order, is the only one which is declared to be absolutely new: "Hitherto have ye asked nothing in my name." Old Testament saints had never known this high privilege, nor had even New Testament disciples, however favored with more advanced knowledge and clearer revelation of divine things, ever yet prayed in Jesus' name.

And for an obvious reason: not until our Lord became God manifest in the flesh, and by his own perfect humanity became identified with our human nature, could the believer have known this glorious truth—that, being by his divinity one with God, and by his humanity one with us, we in Him become one also with God.

The keynote of this lesson is, therefore, the mutual identity of Christ and his disciples. All the precious representations of the unity existing between the believer and his Lord were reserved for the period of his Incarnation: the sevenfold exhibition of that unity found in the seven magnificent figures or symbols employed, is entirely and exclusively found in the New Testament, namely: The Sheep and Shepherd, the Vine and Branches, the Building and Living Stones, the Body and Members, the Family and Head, or larger family of the Commonwealth and Citizens, the Bridegroom and Bride, and that highest conception of all, "He that is joined to the Lord is ONE SPIRIT " (1 Cor. 6. 17.)— all these without exception had to wait for the birth, death, resurrection and ascension of Christ, and the coming of the Holy Ghost, to make them plain or apprehensible. Even the Old Testament foreshadowings of this unity, "He shall feed his flock like a shepherd," (Isaiah 40. 2.) "As a young man marrieth a virgin, so shall thy God rejoice over thee," (Isaiah 62. 5.) "I will sing a song, ... touching my vineyard," (Isaiah 5. 1.) are but fore-shadowing's—enigmatic parables awaiting an interpreter, hieroglyphs awaiting a Champollion. And, even when thus 'adumbrated' in the older gospel. Of the Law and Prophets, they are not used there to exhibit the relation of Christ to the believer, as there in the New Testament. Here, then, was a lesson absolutely new, never taught, certainly never learned, before. How fitting, then, for that closing lesson, to which nothing remains to be added!

First of all, in the closer examination of these words we must not lose sight of the sevenfold repetition of the statement within the compass of this one discourse of our Lord. (John 14, 15,16.)

John 14. 13. Whatsoever ye shall ask in my name, that will I do, that the Father may be glorified in the Son.

John 14. 14. If ye shall ask anything in my name, I will do it.

15. 16. That, whatsoever ye shall ask of the Father in my name, He may give it you.

16. 23. Verily, verily, I say unto you, whatsoever ye shall ask the Father in my name, He will give it you.

24. Hitherto have ye asked nothing in my name. Ask (i.e., in my name) and ye shall receive, that your joy may be full.

26. At that day ye shall ask in my name.

Surely there must be an object in such repetition. Our Lord must have meant especial emphasis to be laid on this new and most advanced lesson.

In this same discourse He explains the ground of this new privilege and right:

John 14. 20. At that day ye shall know that I am in my Father and ye in me and I in you.

15. 7. If ye abide in me and my words abide in you, ye shall ask what ye will and it shall be done unto you.

16. 26, 27. And I say not unto you that I will pray the Father for you, for the Father Himself loveth you because ye have loved me, and have believed that I came out from God.

Compare also our Lord's Intercessory Prayer, (John 17. 9-1 1, 14, 20-26.) where this identity of Christ and believers is further set forth.

This sevenfold lesson teaches us that the union existing between the believer and the Lord Jesus is so complete that there is a mutual indwelling and abiding; so that it is not even needful that the Lord Jesus shall pray for us, since the Father himself recognizes this union between us and His Son, identifies us with him, and loves us for his sake. We are thus in God's sight one with Jesus, whom He heareth always and in whom He is ever well pleased.

How inadequately do all previous teachings and types forecast such fact and privilege! Ahasuerus, handing over the imperial signet-ring to Mordecai and Esther, said: "Write as it liketh you in the King's name, and seal it with the King's ring; for the writing which is written in the King's name and sealed with the King's ring may no man reverse." (Esther 8. 8.) The proclamation that thus went out was in every respect the King's own decree. What they did in his name, he did through them. And our Lord actually conveys to us the signet-ring of God—bids us ask what we will, and seal our prayer with God's own signet. Prayer thus becomes authoritative, like a divine decree.

We have only to turn to the visions of the Apocalypse (Rev. 8. 1-8.) to see this same truth gloriously robed in apocalyptic metaphor. "There was a silence in heaven about the space of half an hour"—as though to prepare for some new and wonderful disclosure. Then our great High Priest appears, offering up the prayers of saints in his own golden censer, perfumed with his own infinite merit; and then, mingling them with that 'fire of the altar' which is the symbol of the power of God, he hurls them back to the earth like thunderbolts, to produce convulsions in the world, and consternation among the enemies of the faith. Prayers that rise up to God in the name of Jesus come back in answers of divine power, comforting saints and bringing dismay to sinners.

This last lesson of Identity with Christ is thus the richest lesson on prayer ever taught, even by our Lord himself. Yet even this may, like the previous lessons, find illustration, if not explanation, in the approach of the High Priest to the mercy-seat.

God is "of purer eyes than to behold evil, and cannot look upon iniquity." What then can give boldness in approaching the thick darkness where God dwells? The right of the High Priest to come unto God at all was found in the blood which he bore, and which served to identify him with the sacrifice for sin: the blood was the life, and, in presenting the blood, he presented the innocent life, the atoning merit and vicarious efficacy of the Lamb of God which it represented.

Our Lord's exact words must be studied: "whatsoever ye shall ask IN MY NAME." The Name stands for the Person, whom it separates, individualizes, distinguishes from all others; consequently to ask in the name of Christ is to ask by virtue of my identity with Christ himself.

It is plain that, when I do or ask anything in another's name, the real actor, the real asker, is not myself, but the other party, who is recognized behind me as my authority in the action or the re-quest. When, in Christ's name—because by faith I am one with him—I come to God and ask, God recognizes Him, not myself, as the actual suppliant. Hence He is. presented as our Intercessor at God's right hand, and as offering or presenting the prayers of His saints on the golden altar and in the golden censer, before the throne; and even as praying to the Father for us or in our behalf.

Thus we reach a fitting climax to this most wonderful series of lessons on prayer. We reach here the highest level of prayer—prayer in Jesus' name. And we come back, at last, to the same essential lesson as at the beginning. The secret of prevailing prayer is the knowledge of God which brings us into sympathy and identity with Him. We can only pray aright as we are in union with all the persons of the trinity: with God the Father, as His obedient children; with God the Holy Spirit, as attuned to His divine mind and will and fitted to be responsive to His inward touch; with God the Son, as identified by faith with his own person and so able to ask in his name.

And now what remains but to learn that consummate practical lesson that touches life at every point: that, like some mighty motive power that lies neglected, waiting to be attached to the vast machinery of manufacture, Prayer in Jesus' Name is the unused force for the individual and church life, the motor equal to all the demands of our spiritual machinery. To many a disciple such prayer is yet in all but name an unknown, untried force, unconnected with the real activities of life. Consequently much work is done in the energy of the flesh that might be done in the energy of the Spirit; much is not done at all that might be attempted and accomplished; and much that is done, and apparently successfully, is only a deceptive superficial achievement which shows no power but man's and yields no glory to God.

We have felt driven onward in writing this book, as by a mighty tidal wave of conviction, that the one all-sufficient and all-comprehensive solution of individual and social problems is a new resort to believing prayer. Every crisis of the kingdom has so far turned on devout supplication. We try our own methods; we rely on numbers, on wealth, on logic and rhetoric, on organization and enterprise, on enthusiasm and intelligence, on social influence and political prestige, on scholarship and secularism; on everything but the Word of God, the Spirit of God and the prevailing hold of suppliant souls on the horns of God's altar of supplication. Consequently our very strength is our weakness and our success is our failure; when we are most confident and boastful, we have most occasion for humility and self-abasement. Our risk is greatest when we feel most secure. Laodiceanism, with its vain self-satisfaction and blindness to its own destitution, is the state of every Christian or every Church that neglects prayer or does not know its self - revealing and divinely - energizing power.

LORD, TEACH US TO PRAY.

34794600R00056

Made in the USA
Middletown, DE
08 September 2016